# how to really
# parent
## YOUR TEENAGER

## Raising Balanced Teens in an Unbalanced World

### Ross Campbell, M.D.
### WITH ROB SUGGS

W PUBLISHING GROUP
A Division of Thomas Nelson Publishers
*Since 1798*

www.wpublishinggroup.com

Published by W Publishing Group, a Division of Thomas Nelson, Inc., P.O. Box 141000, Nashville, Tennessee 37214.

*W Publishing Group books may be purchased in bulk for educational, business, fund-raising, or sales promotional use. For information, please e-mail SpecialMarkets@ThomasNelson.com.*

**Library of Congress Cataloging-in-Publication Data**

Campbell, Ross, 1936-
    How to really parent your teenager : raising balanced teens in an
unbalanced world / Ross Campbell, with Rob Suggs.
        p. cm.
Includes bibliographical references.
    ISBN 0-8499-4542-9
    1. Parenting—Religious aspects—Christianity. 2. Child rearing—
Religious aspects—Christianity. 3. Parent and teenager—Religious
aspects—Christianity. I. Suggs, Rob. II. Title.
    BV4529.C365 2006
    248.8'45—dc22

                                                                    2005035028

*Printed in the United States of America*

06 07 08 09 10 RRD 8 7 6 5 4 3 2 1

# contents

# foreword

NEVER HAS THERE BEEN A MORE EXCITING—OR MORE challenging—era in which to be (or parent) a teenager. The benefits of living in today's global society are great, but so are the dangers. Across the nation pregnancies, sexually transmitted diseases, abortion, drug use, homicide, and suicide have all become commonplace among teens.

But despite these facts, moms and dads continue to have a dramatic impact on their children. Research shows that parents—not peers—exert the most significant influence in the life of a teen. I deeply believe that the most important impact on the teenager's mood and choices is parental love. Without a sense of parental love, teenagers are more prone to be swept along by the contemporary currents of confusion. In contrast, teenagers who genuinely feel loved by their parents are far more likely to respond to the deep longings for community; to welcome structure; to respond positively to guidelines; and to find purpose and meaning in life. Nothing holds more potential for positively changing Western culture than parental love.

If the teenager's emotional need for love is met, it will profoundly affect the behavior of the teenager. At the root of much teenage misbehavior is the teen's empty love tank. I am not suggesting that parents do not love their teenagers; I am suggesting that thousands of teenagers do not feel that love. For most parents it is not a matter of sincerity but rather a lack of information on how to effectively communicate love on an emotional level. Dr. Campbell has helped hundreds of thousands of parents learn how to do this effectively. This book provides for a new generation of parents the insights and skills necessary for effectively meeting the teenager's need for emotional love.

Learning how to process anger in a positive way is a second vital area in which the teenager needs parental influence. Every teenager experiences anger. Unfortunately, some never learn how to respond constructively to the heated emotion of anger. These are the teenagers who eventually commit acts of violence about which we read in the daily news. The successful parent must find a way to help the teenager learn to process anger constructively. For those parents who never learned to handle their own anger, this can be a formidable challenge.

As a psychiatrist with more than thirty years' experience working with troubled teens and their parents, Dr. Ross Campbell is uniquely qualified to write on the subject of anger management. In *How to Really Parent Your Teenager*, Dr. Campbell gives parents the insights necessary to understand teenage anger and a plan for helping teenagers learn how to control their anger rather than being controlled by it.

Keeping your teenager's emotional "love tank" full and helping him or her learn how to manage anger constructively are the foundational stones for successful parenting of teenagers in the twenty-first century. If these two foundation stones are in place, the other aspects of parenting teens will seem like cream on top of the cake. Without these two foundations, the cake will crumble. In *How to Really Parent Your Teenager*, Dr. Campbell gives contemporary parents the recipe for successfully baking the cake and enjoying the "cream."

Gary D. Chapman, PhD.
Author, *The Five Love Languages*
President, Marriage & Family Life Consultants, Inc.
Winston-Salem, North Carolina
www.garychapman.org

# 1

# a stranger in the house

ONE MORE LONG DAY IS OVER. YOU CRAWL UNDER THE BED covers to claim a few hours of rest—one of life's pleasant little rewards. Today you've earned it.

As you click off the lights, your thoughts settle into the comfort of darkness and wander sleepily through the current events of your life. The pace is manageable just now. Bills are paid; plans are progressing; kids are healthy.

Still, a spark of anxiety flickers in the back of your mind. It prevents your calm descent into slumber. That's the parental intuition light, blinking to tell you there is unfinished business somewhere in your family life. Best to ignore it. Think too much about those things and you won't sleep—and that would be unfair to the full day tomorrow.

But you do know what it's all about, don't you? It's something in the air—audible, actually. The faint sound of music creeps down the hall and through your bedroom door. The melody is muffled by earphones, almost unnoticeable. But the rattle of hip-hop percussion is audible in the midnight stillness.

That would be your teenager.

When does he ever sleep, other than at wake-up time in the morning? Aw, well—so much for your own slumber. Now these thoughts can't be blotted out. You sit up and sigh.

*Teenager.* That word alone evokes so many different feelings and questions. You turn the lights back on and allow your thoughts to come forward and speak.

The first thought asks, *Where did the time go?* It almost seems as if you went to the hospital one day, brought home your new-born, filled the photo album with pictures of your "new" family—and already your child was moving rapidly through grade school. Life accelerated in fast-forward mode. His infanthood, toddler-hood, and early childhood slipped from your loving arms far too quickly, one after the other, though you enjoyed each new age and stage. The funny thing about it is that in adult time, only a short season has passed. (For the sake of this illustration, we'll consider your child a male this time.) You look, think, and feel mostly the same way you did a decade and a half ago. That same brief period has represented a lifetime for your child. It was exciting when he learned to walk. You were thrilled when conversation became pos-sible. Starting kindergarten was a wonderful day.

But isn't there some way to pause and enjoy things a bit before he rushes off to college, marriage, parenting, supplying your grandchildren?

That was the first thought. Another one steps forward to ask, *Where did my sweet child go?* All too well you remember a happy, carefree toddler, trying for all he was worth to manage two halting steps across the floor. Or learn the nuances of speech. Or play well with others. Every day was an adventure for your son—but an adventure you shared together.

Again, it seems as if time broke in during the night and stole something precious from you. One morning you awoke to find that your little one was gone—replaced by this tall, gangly, verbally hesitant youth who eats, sleeps, and comes and goes according to strange rules apparently known only to himself or others of his species. *He is so private.* His personality seems as intentionally muffled as the music trapped in those earphones. As a matter of fact, his bedroom door, his stereo, his clothing, his conversation, even the look in his eye—all of these carry one consistent message: *Private property. Keep out.*

And therefore, the next thought interjects: *Where did our tightness go?* That's the only word to describe it: our *tightness.* Our *thing.* This is the big one: the observation that robs you of sleep sometimes.

Your son has been the great joy of your life since he first invaded your world, a little bundle of demands in diapers. What a sensation: a tiny person who placed his entire trust in you. When you walked across the room, his eyes followed you with absorption. You laughed and played together and couldn't tell which one of you was having the best time. Sharing a storybook at bedtime was a priceless treasure. Just hearing his prayers, tucking him in, and kissing him good night brought you a deep sense of emotional fulfillment. You can remember realizing, *This is what my life is about. Being a parent is the center of my universe.*

So what's going on? No great canyon has opened in the earth to pull you two apart. You are still friends, still parent and child, and he still depends on you. His love for you is assured. But for the first time, things are not at all the same. Your child has entered that uncertain twilight world between childhood and adulthood. He isn't certain how to navigate its strange waters. You want to help, but you don't have all the answers or even his permission to submit them.

Somewhere around his thirteenth birthday, the child you knew began to retreat into a very personal world to try to work it all out for himself. When you made an effort to follow him there, you encountered a tension that was entirely new; messages that said, "Leave me alone. Let me do this myself."

And you knew instinctively that some of that was simply the way of things. It was, after all, a stage you remembered from your own life.

> **Your child has entered that uncertain twilight world between childhood and adulthood.**

But there are limits, aren't there? You knew it, and you still know it. Parental love must find a way to prevail even when it is pushed away. Your child continues to have needs you must fulfill, same as ever. Imagine leaving him alone, becoming a hands-off parent. Who knows? He might not even get up and go to school. He might not leave his room at all. Or he might leave it forever. He could make disastrous decisions. Just that thought alone is enough to have you up past midnight, alone with your fears.

It all comes down to these unshakable truths:

* You are a parent.
* You love your child.

- You want him to become a young adult of maturity, confidence, and integrity.
- You are willing to pay whatever price is necessary to attain that goal.

You have begun to realize you have to find ways to remain a guiding force in your child's life; a way to slip in past the "Keep Out" signs, the earphones, and the unspoken fashion and cultural signals that say, "I am different now. I've outgrown the storybooks, and I don't need to be tucked in anymore. Let's just peacefully coexist."

> **Parenting and "peaceful coexistence" don't go together.**

Parenting and "peaceful coexistence" don't go together.

These are the current events of the world that is your home—the emotional environment of one particular family. But there's something else that keeps you awake too. Your mind turns from the world within to the world without. For that's a great part of your anxiety, isn't it? For the first time, the outside world is part of the equation. Here lie the threats that often make you feel powerless. The world is changing rapidly, and most of us are very concerned about the quality of those changes.

## Our Changing World

Sure, change is an all-the-time thing—always has been, always will be. The only thing about the world that *never* changes is that it *always* changes. But these past few decades have been something altogether different. You and I have lived through a time of disruptive, almost seismic cultural transition. The second half of the twentieth century is often called "Culture Shock"—the phenomenon of a society that undergoes a cultural evolution more rapid than our ability to adjust to it. Think of the technological innovations that have transformed your world in the lifetime of your child alone. Can you remember a time when people could drive, shop, and take simple walks without chattering into cell phones? When there was no computer in your home? When your television had three channels, and all of them were G-rated?

Can you remember when love songs were corny and sentimental rather than racy and anatomical? Can you remember when public leaders were revered rather than ridiculed, and athletes were heroes rather than villains?

Some of these changes are fairly innocuous or even exciting. Cell phones are good for safety, and the Internet enhances our possibilities in education and communication. But we've all recognized changes that are more insidious in nature. Let's examine a few of them in the light of your mission as a parent.

## The Permeation of Mass Media

Electronic information and entertainment were once a relatively small part of daily life. During World War II, people got their daily news on a delayed basis over the radio. People enjoyed popular music, perhaps bought a few recordings, and attended the movies. But in today's world, mass media drive the culture. We've seen the dawn of the Internet generation; just as many of us made up the television generation.

Being "wired" to pop culture is very important to today's adolescents. Pollster George Barna identifies two key elements that teenagers consider essential to their daily experience: relationships and mass-media experience.[1] Kids are very conscious of their connection to the greater world. Movies, music, TV shows, and Web sites are much more than diversions to them; they are part of life's structure.

Just as teens are more tuned in to mass media, the media themselves are far more intrusive to our lives. We have opened ourselves up to the media, of course, in our habits as a consumer society. Many of us have several televisions and computers in the home. We build our family time around the dictates of *TV Guide*. We abhor the state of sex and violence in films, but we seem to make those movies successful at the box office. To some extent it could be said that a society gets the entertainment it deserves. But we need to be concerned about this mass-media–driven culture and its ability to shape our children's values.

## The Saturation of Sexual Obsession

That same mass media, of course, brings pictures and language into our homes that we would not have believed possible even two decades ago. The period from eight o'clock to ten o'clock at night was once an inviolable sanctuary for the family audience—the domain of heartwarming family-situation comedies and musical variety shows. Now it offers scenes that would once have earned an R-rating in movie theaters. Pop music, with younger teens as the target audience, focuses on sexual titilla-

> **The Internet can potentially give sexual predators the key to your home.**

tion, and its stars rise according to the appeal of their bodies rather than their voices.

At the same time, the Internet can potentially give sexual predators the key to your home—if you're not a vigilant gatekeeper. That, of course, is our central consideration in safeguarding our children: doing all that we can to supervise what is admitted to the eyes and ears of impressionable children in our homes.

## The Victory of Materialism

Psychologist Patricia Dalton says that rampant consumerism has America in its clutches. She observes unhappy people trying to fill the emptiness of their lives by spending more and more. They come to her to find out why it has all gone wrong.

"Those of us who lived through the '60s," she says, "seem to have forgotten the warning that everything you buy owns you." Consumers pursue the latest plasma televisions, digital video recorders, and iPods. They stretch their financial capabilities to buy the dream house. Then, to pay for the house, they work so hard that they destroy the home.[2] Tension grows in families as the sea of financial debt grows deeper. At the same time, our children pick up our materialistic values. Meanwhile, the mass-media world, driven as it is by consumerism, persuades them that if they spend, spend, spend, then everything will be all right.

## The Spread of Violence

We all know about Columbine and the rise of youthful violence. While there is no public consensus about the main cause of this trend, it is a fact of our children's lives that their schools are now monitored by closed-circuit cameras more often than not;

their lockers are regularly searched for handguns and narcotics. Bullying is a bigger problem than ever. Gang affiliations are spreading from urban cityscapes to the suburbs, and we have legitimate reasons to take special precautions for our teenagers. But of course, in many cases the problem is in the home itself, via domestic violence. Two million children are seriously injured by parents or guardians each year, and nearly one million parents are beaten or abused by their own children.[3]

The real culprit, as we will see, is the presence of the toxic anger that lies just beneath the surface of our culture today. People in general are angry and frustrated. They haven't been trained to handle their own anger, and they can't train their kids to handle it. Unmanaged emotions make the outbreak of violence an inevitability.

## The Dark Age of Integrity

James Patterson and Peter Kim wrote a book called *The Day America Told the Truth*. Using confidential surveys, they produced a troubling snapshot of the moral climate of this country. Only 13 percent believe in the Ten Commandments—but 40 percent believe in five of them. In other words, Americans make up their own moral codes.[4] We pick and choose from God's laws as we would pick food from a lunch buffet. Lying, they said, is "embedded in our national character."[5]

A dishonest politician once made for front-page headlines— unacceptable public scandal. It could be argued that we expect our officials to lie and bend rules today. Some people seem to have the idea that integrity is no longer practical; it simply doesn't work. Therefore students might as well go ahead and cheat on exams. Business executives falsify their expense reports. And as of 2003, nearly one-quarter of us believed that cheating on our tax returns was all right.[6]

Is it possible to raise children of integrity in a world that no longer believes in such a value? Yes, it certainly is. But we have our work cut out for us.

## The Explosion of Mobility

Did you expect to see mobility listed as a troublesome change in our world? Certainly it can be a wonderful thing. Increased mobility means you can easily visit your old college roommate in Seattle or take your children on a hike through the Scottish Highlands. Our world has shrunk, and our horizons have broadened.

But how many of us can truly say that life, as a whole, is better because of the rapidity with which we move around? How does it affect our children to be frequently uprooted and moved from one city to another? How much do they need regular contact with a loving extended family—a network of aunts, uncles, cousins, grandparents, and friends who have known you all your life?

We should mention here that the church has borne the brunt of change in nearly every category we've listed so far. Mobility may well head the list. Many of us, the parents, grew to adulthood among a congregation of caring people, the ultimate extended family we know as the church. There were pastors, youth directors, and Sunday school teachers who knew us well as we grew and changed. They truly cared about us because they had invested some of their own lives in ours.

At the same time, we learned what it meant to be committed to the local body of Christ—to give our time, our money, and our years in a sacrificial way to build the church body. Many parents today are "church hoppers and shoppers." They move from congregation to congregation, wholly consumers rather than holy communers. What message do our children derive from this? Why are we shocked when they drop out of churchgoing at the first opportunity? Of course, there are other reasons they do so, as we will see in a later chapter.

## And Now for the Good News

As we've seen, it's not difficult to paint a bleak picture of today's parenting environment. So why not just throw our hands up in the air and surrender? Why not move to a gated community and lock our children safely in our carefully sanitized homes until they are young adults?

Because believe it or not, there is good news too; there always is, even when times are darkest. I want to encourage you to be upbeat and positive in the face of today's challenges, and I want you to consider the "upside" of raising a teenager effectively in the modern world.

Today's teens are healthier and better educated than any in our history. They are more likely to attend college. They are more likely to get involved in community service projects and mission endeavors. While they may not connect to the church in the same patterns or approaches as their parents and grandparents have, they are extremely interested in spiritual issues, and—if we can get them involved—they will take their faith quite seriously and make the church a better place.

> **Today's teens are healthier and better educated than any in our history.**

This is a very angry generation. But that anger can be trained and channeled into emotional and spiritual maturity. This is a media-obsessed generation. But that interest can be channeled into a better, healthier media culture if we help our children see from a biblical perspective.

**This is a generation God loves.**

This is a generation challenged by materialism, violence, and integrity issues. But every one of those items can become a powerful, life-shaping teaching point in the hands of a good parent who knows how to communicate.

Finally, this is a generation God loves. We could say that, of course, about every generation in world history. But it helps us to be reminded that God still watches over this world. Our kids may exasperate us sometimes, but they never push themselves beyond the bounds of his love and patience. We may run out of answers sometimes, but God never does.

The writer of Ecclesiastes concluded, "What has been will be again, what has been done will be done again; there is nothing new under the sun" (1:9). Today's problems may seem very new and very different, and from our perspective they are. But the basic human condition never changes, and neither do the needs of every young person. When you come to the very edge of your endurance and wisdom, remember that God's resources are infinite; that no human being has yet presented a problem for which he has no answer; that the finest steel has to be tempered by a certain amount of fire. But once that tempering has taken place, the steel is powerful enough to pass even the harshest tests. Your child can be like that someday.

Remember also, during these toughest of times, that the basic needs are really very simple. Your teen needs to experience unconditional love and feel profoundly secure. He needs to learn to manage anger and the wide array of emotions that come with adolescence. He needs to learn his place in the world beyond your front door. And he needs to complete the foundation of his personhood that you have strived to help him lay since the day he was born. When the day comes that you can smile and acknowledge you have raised a balanced teen even in an unbalanced world, you'll know you can spend the rest of your life with a large sense of satisfaction—mission accomplished. You will have made a powerful contribution to the future of this world and of the kingdom of God.

These are great tasks for you as a parent—heroic tasks, actually. You will need wisdom, patience, guidance, and perseverance. But what could be a greater goal than leaving the world the legacy of a child you have poured all of yourself into preparing? I know you've already discovered—and would still admit even during the worst moments—that there is no greater and more satisfying task in life than that of being a good parent. It could also be said that there is no greater and more satisfying part of parenting than right now—the borderline years between childhood and adulthood— the time we have come to call adolescence.

## A Road Map for Our Journey

I hope and pray that this book will become an essential companion for your challenge of being the parent of a teenager. There's no way to deal with every issue and every question that will arise during your own journey, but I believe we can confront the most essential ones. Let's examine the "road map" of the places we'll be going and the main stops we'll be making in this book.

- In the second and third chapters, we will face what I believe to be the greatest danger of all for our children: the nemesis of anger. It's my contention that anger has quietly enslaved our world because a generation has grown up without good training in how to manage it. The results may seem to be the equivalent of a few temper tantrums in your living room, but they are in fact much greater. The bitter fruit of unacknowledged, unmanaged anger is a life that will spiral increasingly out of control—straight on through the rites of school, relationships, work, marriage, and parenting—until it spirals back upon its bearer, toward self-destruction. There is also the issue of the parent's anger, which can add terrible and destructive complications to the task we face. Parents and teens alike can be angry, but they can also manage that anger maturely. This subject of anger is so important that we will discuss it first off in the next chapter.

- The fourth and fifth chapters bring us a more positive topic: love, the foundation of all good parenting. There are specific challenges to loving a teenager. For example, how can we overtly and physically express our affection for someone who hides in the bedroom or wants only to be with friends? How can we love them when they are sarcastic and insolent? In particular, how do we create the right kind of home atmosphere of unconditional love and acceptance when a teenager has changed that atmosphere so drastically? At this very point many parents go astray from proper techniques and attitudes. They withhold love out of frustration, or they become discouraged by the "don't touch me" signals and stop trying to show their love. Chapter 4 presents the concept of unconditional love in the home, and the following chapter explores the three primary ways you can provide love to your teenager. We'll discover some helpful approaches that will make your home a warm and positive outpost not only for your children, but for their friends.

- What about discipline? For many of my past readers, this has been the greatest of all questions—and for good reason. There is tremendous confusion on this point in today's world. For one thing, the entire definition of the word is misunderstood; people believe *discipline* and *punishment* are synonymous. Do our children need more of the old-fashioned "hard-line" discipline, with a "spare the rod and spoil the child" philosophy? Or should we take a laissez-faire "hands-off" approach that allows teenagers to set the tone and the rules? As you have guessed, both of these strategies can have disastrous consequences. But where is the right road? We'll find it in Chapter 6 on disciplining teenagers.

- The seventh chapter will focus on protecting your child in the jungle of today's tangled world. We've already examined some of the symptoms of the new culture that confronts us. Its ideas, philosophies, and illusions are in the very cultural air our children breathe. There is no way to keep a teenager from being exposed to wrong attitudes and even certain dangerous potential situations (in the schools, for example). But we can take many proactive steps. And we can also help our children see this world through the lens of wisdom, of both the biblical and commonsense varieties, so that they eventually reject the disastrous ways the world teaches. We want them to decide, for example, that premarital sexual experience is very foolish, rather than the normal course the world presents it to be. We want them to make healthy choices in the music they listen to and the shows they watch, even after we are no longer around to help them decide. This chapter helps us build walls of protection for our most precious resources, our children.

- In the eighth chapter we'll take a special look at the media-saturated world in which our children live. We need to understand the new realities of the "techno-teens," who have no precedent in world history. Just as baby boomers were molded to some extent by the preeminence of television, the new generation is very much part of the information age. The nonlinear "hypertext" world of the Internet, for example, has already been shown to be a powerful influence in causing younger people to reason differently. If you want to truly love and understand the mind of your child, you must know the context. We'll take a look at it in this chapter.

- Training in sexuality is essential, and our ninth chapter will offer some guidance in taking on this crucial task. There was a time when parents could speak to their children on this subject without competition. Unfortunately, our children are hearing the world's views of sexuality in all the wrong places, well before the age we would desire for them to be trained. How can we counteract this? Also, what do we need to teach our children about gender differences in general?

- What about spiritual training? Naturally, we haven't left that subject out of our book. Chapter 10 is devoted to spiritual formation in the home. We will explore practical issues of faith development. Most of us have made the observation that many young people walk away from the church as soon as they leave home. Why is this? How can we grow faith in our children so that the seeds take root and bear a blossom that won't wither? Then we need to consider the subject of church, which I've observed much more closely over the past few years, on a professional basis. Many churches and ministers are in great pain today—and too often you and I are at the root of the problem. It is possible to teach our teenagers good churchmanship. We'll find ways you and your child can be supportive of the work of your church—and particularly of the youth programs.

- We have seen outbreaks of anxiety and depression among adolescents in our time. All kinds of behavioral disorders have become household words, particularly in the context of teenagers. In the eleventh chapter we'll take a practical look at how to approach these problems, how to know the warning signs, and how to be assured that our children have the best opportunity to be healthy and happy.

- Finally, let's take a positive look at the legacies we can be working now to leave for our teenagers and their future.

- A special study guide has been added to either help you use this book in a group setting or to maximize your personal study.

As you can see, we have a lot of ground to cover! I pray our discussion will be positive, uplifting, and inspiring to you in your quest to be an excellent parent. Let's get started.

# anger: the essential problem

IMAGINE FOR A MOMENT A WORLD WITHOUT ANGER. WOULD YOU want to live there?

When news came of a terrible crime, there would be no anger. When a politician revealed he had betrayed the public trust, there would be no outrage. If an African-American church was bombed by a racist group, people would only shrug.

Anger is a necessary part of the human constitution. Many great advances in our history have come as a result of someone's *righteous* anger (the qualifier is very important). Slavery was abolished because someone became angry about it. Women received the right to vote for the same reason. Our nation exists because its founding fathers acted upon their outrage over excessive taxation and other unjust policies. Anger is a great asset, but yes—it can also be a great problem. I believe that anger may present the most dangerous single challenge your children are facing today.

What is anger exactly? It is an emotional state that comes in varying proportions, according to the situation and the individual's capacity for the emotion. Anger is a physical and psychological response to a threat of some kind. We know that it stimulates a number of bodily responses: elevated heart rate and blood pressure, energy hormones, adrenaline, and noradrenaline.[1]

Anger can be caused by an infinite variety of sources; the responses can take an infinite variety of forms. Anger can even seem to be invisible in both cause and effect, particularly if it is repressed by the one who feels it or it is suppressed by others. That's when anger becomes truly dangerous.

**Anger has become a problem of epic proportions in our current culture.**

Clearly, then, anger is all around us. You have felt your share of it, and so have those close to you. Take a look around your business office or the aisles of the grocery store, and you are likely to see someone who shows all the signs of feeling some kind of anger. What you'll notice is how often people express their anger toward something or someone who is not its cause. A coworker snaps at you by the watercooler, and you're certain the cause had nothing to do with you—you were just in the wrong place at the wrong time.

As I stated earlier, I believe anger has become a problem of epic proportions in our current culture. This is an angry world. Just listen to the radio, watch a supposed "comedy" show on television, listen to the songs being played on contemporary radio stations, or simply take notice wherever you go. I think you'll agree with me that there is a great deal of simmering emotion, and almost none of it is related to the place or situation where it is being expressed. For example, that driver on the freeway who showed rudeness that was totally out of proportion (not that there is a proper "proportion" for rudeness)—was it truly your seemingly inoffensive driving that sent him over the edge, or was it something in his personal world? Surely the latter.

I think you can see the point. If anger is frequently being expressed at the improper time and place—and usually in an improper fashion—then we find ourselves living in a world of irrational events. But that's probably not news to any of us. This chapter aims to accomplish two goals:

1. To identify the forms anger will take in the life of your teenager.
2. To establish strategies for managing and diffusing anger.

## How Anger Operates

Anger is a jolt to the human system. It naturally seeks an outlet. A small child is playing with his mother's cell phone, and Mommy takes it away. The child will cry or vent her emotions in some way. Anger doesn't like being contained—not when we are children or adults. As we grow older, the causes and expressions of our anger grow more complex. Many factors affect your teenager's emotions, many of which will pass beneath your parental radar. Just be conscious that anger is normal, inevitable, and appears regularly.

Adolescents are still children in important ways, and their emotions outpace their capabilities to verbalize them. But scientists have recently pinpointed a phenomenon that takes place in the teenage brain at the outset of adolescence. There is an unexpected growth spurt in the frontal cortex, an overproduction of cells just before puberty. It is the first such wave of overproduction since the child was in the womb. The ability to plan, create strategies, and be organized will not come until later. For now, there is a powerful surge of emotional forces but little practical ability to regulate them. This is one of the reasons we have all observed teenagers to be disorganized, sloppy, and ill-planned. Creativity, surging emotions, hormones, and other factors are kicking in—but the brain's "CEO" or administration resources are simply not ready.[2]

So there is a jumble of disorganized emotions. A primary emotion is anger. Your daughter may be angry at some trifle, yet it seems to you that she is angrier than she should be. Something deeper is the problem, possibly something totally unrelated. How are you going to handle this situation?

First, consider the preeminent issue regarding anger. What is most important? The cause, of course. Second, find out the problem, tend to it, and the emotions will disperse. But life is never that simple, of course. For one thing, these crises always intrude on everyday life, just when you're busy with other tasks and anxieties. It's difficult to stop in your tracks and engage every problem in the life of your child. It's difficult to even *identify* the problems. Bottom line: we find ourselves dealing with the symptom rather than the cause.

Consider how often you may have focused on the *expression* of anger rather than its subject. For example, you may be so taken aback by your daughter's insolent tone that you will forget entirely what might have set off her reaction. You have asked her to clear the papers off the sofa in the television room, to which she responded with a sarcastic remark. "I never talked to my parents that way," you say. Then you offer your description of exactly what would have happened if you had given your parents any "back talk." You've offered it several times in the past, of course.

By this time you're not thinking at all about whatever is the root of the problem. You are regarding the problem of disrespect of parents. Then your teenager becomes even more frustrated because your response is just another problem for her, another reason to be angry.

Please note that the teen's behavior may indeed be unacceptable. She could pick up the papers without protest. But that's not the issue. Sarcastic rejoinders are unpleasant and unacceptable; neither is *that* the issue.

There is something, large or small, that made your teenager angry. In this case, we later discover that your daughter is angry because her three best friends will be at the mall that evening, and she isn't allowed to go. It's your policy that she can't go out with friends on a school night. So her source of anger is actually unrelated to cleaning off the sofa. She spouted off because she was thinking about her friends having fun while she tidied a mess. Her inner emotion was: *It's not fair!*

> The main principle of anger management is to look past the symptoms and address the cause.

She has expressed her anger, if inappropriately. Your ultimate goal for her is to understand and manage her emotions, which includes expressing them appropriately. But that will take time and training. It's virtually impossible for any teenager to be a wise and mature handler of unpleasant and painful emotions; it's rare today to find adults who qualify, for that matter.

At this point you are most likely thinking, *But it's always some insignificant thing. There are a million things that might make my daughter angry.* That's true. But let's explore what happens when these minor things aren't properly managed.

## The Many Faces of Anger

The main principle of anger management is to look past the symptoms and address the cause. The final goal is to learn to deal with anger *verbally* and *pleasantly.* An attentive parent can help the teenage son or daughter engage the problem constructively, while gently making it known that certain expressions of anger are unacceptable. No, this is not a simple cure. It's not always possible for everyone to halt in their tracks and investigate the source. And many problems can't be solved in twenty-two minutes, as they were on *Leave It to Beaver* or *Father Knows Best.* No one promised this would be easy. Just the same, we need to remember, as we look past the symptom, to use each situation as a "teachable moment" to help a child on the way toward mature anger management.

When your child is angry, she will express it in at least one of several ways. Please consult the Anger Ladder—the chart at the end of this chapter. I have used it for years to show the progression from immaturity to wisdom as we learn to manage our anger. At the bottom you'll find the worst and most dangerous forms of reaction; the top of the ladder shows our goal. Let's discuss some of the most common expressions of anger.

## Acting Out

The most instinctive human reaction to anger is aggression, and it can take many forms. For teenagers, gone are the tantrums of earlier childhood. But they refine their expressions of aggression to the point of making it a fine art. They act out their emotions through body language such as heavy sighing or facial expressions, sulking, whining, and arguing. They can easily make their parents miserable by these varying actions. They master that precise look in the eye or that irritating inflection of voice. They seem to push all our own anger buttons, and perhaps that's exactly what is happening; anger, like misery, loves company.

As unpleasant as these manifestations may be, they are far from the most damaging expressions of anger. The worst comes when we make the situation worse by overreacting to their reactions. For example, your daughter is upset because she is at home clearing papers off the sofa while her friends chat over a burger at the food court. Even while she snaps at you and looks as if she will spend the evening sulking, at least it's a passing thing. She will have forgotten about tonight's lost trip to the mall by tomorrow. But if you lose your temper, the problem becomes compounded, and her resentment is now directed at you. You bring in the parental respect issue, and now your daughter flees to her room with such parting words as, "Why is the whole world against me?"

Yes, she can be a "drama queen." It's melodramatic and silly from your perspective. But it helps to remember when you once felt that way. You need to remind yourself that maturation is a long process.

Be firm in reminding your child what kind of behavior isn't appropriate, but be gentle. The biblical proverb tells us that "a gentle answer turns away wrath" (Proverbs 15:1). Much of the time, a ready ear and a show of understanding will defuse these simpler expressions of anger. You'll spare yourself the worst of the acting out, and you'll model a mature perspective to your child.

## Venting

Did we say the tantrums of an earlier age are gone? Not always. People of all ages are known to give full ventilation to their anger at times. Since teenagers experience turbulent emotions, they may well "let off some steam" on occasion: slamming a door, throwing a book or some other object, yelling, or even acting violently toward someone. Needless to say, venting is unacceptable. While facial expressions, heavy sighing, and sarcastic intonations merely annoy us, venting cannot be permitted.

I'm often asked, "But isn't it healthy to slam a few doors? Isn't it better for me to scream at someone in the family and get it all out of my system? After all, it's far less healthy to keep all this turmoil pent up inside me."

That last statement may have a shred of truth. As we will see in the next section, the most deadly form of anger is indeed the kind that has been pent up, only to emerge in an irrational form later. But there is a great myth that "we all need to vent." One billboard, for example, says, "Hit a pillow, hit the wall, but don't hit your kid." While we commend the message against child abuse, the offered alternative isn't an example of mature anger management.

Some define venting as simply talking about their anxieties. That's a good thing—as a matter of fact, pleasantly verbalizing our feelings is the ultimate goal. But the traditional understanding of ventilation—giving free rein to runaway emotions—is a more serious matter. For one thing, contrary to popular opinion, ventilation does not clear the air. In an experiment performed many years ago—but the results of which are still valid in our world today—workers were given stinging insults. Then, half of them were allowed to pound on nails with a hammer for ten minutes. The other half wasn't given that opportunity. At the end of the experiment, everyone was allowed to talk about the one who insulted them. Was the hammer crowd more docile? Just the opposite. The nail-hitters were more worked up than ever![3]

Many experiments have confirmed this finding: venting doesn't put out fires, it pours gasoline onto them. Unrestrained anger is the proverbial bull in the china shop, disruptive and dangerous for several reasons. It creates poor behavioral precedents that can become patterns. It becomes rage. It can inflict physical damage. Listen to the wisdom of Scripture: "A fool gives full vent to his anger, but a wise man keeps himself under control" (Proverbs 29:11). Surely that's better than the conventional wisdom about "letting off steam."

As a parent you should think carefully about your own venting. If you tend to let your anger fly, that's a habit your children are certain to imitate.

## Repression and Suppression

Sometimes the anger is stifled completely. *Repression* is the opposite of venting: we "push it all back in" for some reason. If a policeman is writing you a traffic ticket, you're not likely to give your anger free rein. Fear is the most basic reason anyone might cover up feelings of anger. Suppression is when someone else prevents us from expressing our feelings. Since we're discussing your task as a parent, this is the definition we want to explore in greater detail.

Suppression occurs when one person or group has greater power over another, as in the case of parent and child. Any good parent suppresses his or her children to some extent, and particularly early in the child's life. Otherwise they would be irresponsible parents. You don't allow your child to cross the street alone or to eat all the cookies he wants to eat. But as your child reaches adolescence, your power must be exercised with a good bit more thought and consideration. Your teenager will test the boundaries, finding out just how far she can go in her speech or her behavior. Knowing where to draw the line is no easy task.

> **If you learn to rely on suppression, you will win all the battles but resoundingly lose the war.**

When your child is acting out, arguing, whining, and disrupting the household, you must decide how to defuse the latest crisis. How much anger should you suppress? And how? Leveraging your power to silence an angry teen will bring about two results:

1. It will make things quiet for the time being.
2. It will keep the fire of anger flickering inside your child.

If you learn to rely on suppression, you will win all the battles but resoundingly lose the war. Let's discover why by returning to the case of the daughter and the lost trip to the mall.

## Is That Your Final Answer?

Your daughter is storming through the television room. She's carrying out the task you requested, but she's making everyone miserable in the process—muttering under her breath, picking things up and tossing them aside angrily, and looking to pick a fight with her younger brother. How are you going to handle this situation?

First, let's imagine you come into the room, raise your voice, and demand that your daughter "clean up her act." You've had a hard day, you tell her, and she is treading on your last nerve strand. Your daughter rolls her eyes and says something insolent. Now comes the lecture about how kids were once afraid to act out this way. Your daughter, of course, will not immediately clean up her act. Teenagers cannot handle anger maturely. Your daughter was previously angry about the mall; now she is angry about the mall, your lecture, and little brother, who just tattled on her. Anger is a rolling stone that gathers moss.

More words are exchanged; now comes the moment of decision—the moment that reveals your parenting skills.

Here are some things you might say:

- "Okay, okay! Do you have any idea how impossible you are to live with lately?"
- "Go to your room and think about the way you've been acting."
- "Not another word about it! Why? Because I said so!"
- "Time out. Arguing won't get us anywhere. Let's take a moment to cool down, then we can calmly sort things out."

Which of these statements would most likely be heard in your home? Which do you think is the wisest approach? Which is the worst option?

Clearly, the fourth statement is on the right track. The third is the least advisable, particularly if those words are said frequently.

Why? Suppression of talk suggests that the parent is low on listening skills. When communication fails and anger is unmanaged, the great danger is passive-aggressive anger. While this term is often thrown around with some lack of precision, the concept is extremely important. Let's clearly define what passive-aggressive anger is, and why you should avoid it.

## Stealth Anger: The Passive-Aggressive Enigma

As we've stated, suppressing unpleasant behavior provides a quiet room but doesn't dispose of the anger. Anger seeks expression; it can't be simply swept under the rug.

Anger must be directly managed to be defused. This isn't usually what we want to hear or face, but think about this carefully. You can deal with the situation right now, while you're tired and the anger is limited and rational; or you can deal with it sometime in the future, when the repressed/suppressed anger has become more intense and irrational. Therapists developed the idea of passive-aggressive (PA) anger, which is a misdirected and irrational emotional response. It is characterized by the expression of negative feelings, resentment, and aggression in an unassertive way—most typically procrastination, stubbornness, and a lack of willingness to communicate.

But in recent times this term has been overused and often misused until its meaning has become blurry in some people's minds. To differentiate my own understanding of passive aggression as it relates specifically to anger, I have used the term "stealth anger." In the military, stealth technology and stealth missiles fly beneath radar detection. Therefore the weapons are stealthy or furtive; they seem to come from nowhere. Stealth anger, then, is furtive, undetected anger whose origins we can't immediately "track." If a person either cannot express and manage anger in a healthy way, then the anger stays in the subconscious until it can emerge in a disruptive and destructive way.

That kind of anger "goes underground," where it becomes entangled with other unresolved strands of emotion. Ultimately, stealth anger will express itself in many damaging and long-term ways. A teenager with PA anger might show some combination of these symptoms:

- Procrastination: "I'll do it later."
- Unwarranted inefficiency: "I don't know how."
- Irresponsibility: "I forgot."
- Blaming: "It's the teacher's fault."
- Resentment: "They're all like that."
- Sullenness: "I don't want to talk about it."
- Resistance to authority: "I won't work for him."
- Resistance to cooperation or assistance: "I don't need your help."

It's important to be cautious about making your own diagnosis. For one thing, there is a certain period of normal passive-aggressive behavior in early adolescence, and we'll examine it later. Most teenagers can procrastinate and be sullen or irresponsible. These are only the symptoms. Keep in mind that passive-aggressive or stealth anger is existing anger that has been misdirected. The teenager is unlikely to tell you what the real problem is because he probably doesn't know. You can be more certain you're encountering PA behavior if you keep in mind the following characteristics of the behavior, and if you observe them consistently:

1. *Stealth anger is irrational.* For example, your daughter's grades suddenly plummet. She is intelligent and was once an exceptional student, but now she is in danger of dropping out of school. It makes absolutely no sense. All she has to do is try a little harder, yet it does no good to tell her that. The more you tell her, the worse the behavior comes. Stealth anger is irrational in foundation, and it will resist rational solutions.

2. *Stealth anger is targeted at authority.* Misdirected anger always targets the one in charge. If grades are important to you, the parent, then grades are a likely setting for the stealth-anger behavior. If you value church involvement for your whole family, your child may suddenly resist any dealings with the church— even though friends and fun activities are there, and your child has always enjoyed them and will now miss them. Stealth-anger behavior is irrational and is targeted at the central authority.

3. *Stealth anger is ultimately self-inflicted aggression.* Who is the central target when your daughter drops out? *You.* Who will suffer the most? *Your daughter,* because this development will have a tremendously negative effect on her future. Even this truth cannot be rationally argued to your angry child. Remember, it's irrational, and it's all about hurting the authority figure, even at the expense of one's own suffering.

Why are we seeing so many younger people, generally intelligent and from affluent families, behaving irrationally? Some examples might include partaking in school violence, bright kids dropping out of school, drug and alcohol abuse, teenage pregnancy, and shoplifting when money isn't a problem? Though there are other root causes, I believe that passive-aggressive anger is a cultural epidemic today. In the last few decades we've seen a rise in authoritarian discipline, supposedly traditional, punishment-based, and highly suppressive. A generation of children has therefore come along with more than their share of unresolved anger. It's no wonder we see a world filled with antiauthority people in the workplace, the entertainment world, the churches, and everywhere we turn.

> **I believe that passive-aggressive anger is a cultural epidemic today.**

At its core stealth-anger behavior is a refusal to take responsibility for one's own behavior. A suppressive parent has already monopolized the responsibility, preempting it by use of power and authority. That mom or dad is saying, "Your anger is my problem. I am making the decisions about it; your only decision is to stifle your feelings or face consequences." We will talk more about discipline in a later chapter.

## Normal Passive Aggression

I want to emphasize that a certain amount of stealth behavior or passive aggression is normal. You shouldn't be alarmed when you observe it in early adolescence, between the ages of thirteen and fifteen. The younger teenager is developing her self-concept, learning to think abstractly, and figuring out a puzzling world. Typically, younger adolescents begin to dawdle on homework assignments, make excuses about getting chores done, and exhibit other lesser manifestations of this kind of behavior. It is irritating to say the least, but it makes a great difference when we, the parents, can realize that it's just part of the age profile. Then we don't need to hit the panic button.

Handle the situation lovingly and effectively, and this behavior will work itself out in time; handle it ineffectively, and it will spread outside the home to school, neighborhood, and church. The minor, isolated anger will then become a larger, more problematic manifestation. But it begins in the home, where we can handle it and contain it. So how much is normal?

Expect a messy bedroom. Nearly every parent has to cope with this irritation. Talk to other parents and you'll discover you're not alone. But wouldn't you rather be confronted by an untidy room than something more serious—shoplifting or violence, for example? A passive-aggressive male, in his late teenage years, may get involved in breaking into homes; a passive-aggressive female may become sexually promiscuous. These are common results in cases where anger has not been detected and managed at an earlier stage. Obviously, those are much more serious issues with very negative consequences. By comparison, messy bedrooms, unkempt clothing, unfinished homework assignments, and perhaps a temporary dip in grades can be seen as passing annoyances, *if* we find and handle the lesser portions of anger beneath them. Confront the problems, but try not to be heavy-handed and aggravate the anger. Misguided parenting of that type could drive the anger deeper, where it might become more entrenched and possibly surface in more irrational and damaging behavior.

It can be difficult not to overreact at times. My son David allowed his grades to slide from an A or B average to C when he was in eighth grade. I monitored the situation, toughed it out, and tried not to make a big deal out of it. David knew that better grades were expected of him. Two years passed. Believe me, it's difficult for a parent to control his or her reactions for two years! David was in tenth grade and still struggling, and I was worried.

But in the nick of time, our son realized that all his friends were heading to college, and he could be left behind. When he came to me to talk about his future, that was the right time for me to share my observations about his study habits. From that moment on, David was ready to be a good student. He applied himself with tremendous energy, and it all worked out for him. This was a lesson he had to learn for himself, and that couldn't have happened if his mother and I had stood over him every night during homework time, shaking our fists and issuing threats.

This is a lot to ask of you as a parent. How should you react during this trying stage, when your own self-control is so important?

- **Use the "Yogi Bear" speech pattern.** That cartoon character began his sentences with a lower inflection and ended up higher. This is the way mothers talk to little children— it's gentle and noncombative. You would be surprised how much aggression tends to come through our tone of voice otherwise, even when we are measuring our words carefully.
- **Use questions rather than commands.** A sentence like, "Go do your work right now!" shows little respect, and your teenager is very interested in being treated with respect. You might ask, "Homework still on schedule?" The important point here is that the teenager owns the responsibility, not you. Questions acknowledge that ownership, while commands acknowledge that you are in power.
- **Use your eyes.** We often don't see how we look when we are scolding; our eyes seem to be on fire. Sometimes we just give "the evil eye" rather than saying anything at all, and this may be the most dehumanizing treatment of all. Even *averting* eye contact is a bad idea, because that's a message

of nonacceptance. Concentrate on the gentle, loving look
that your eyes can convey.

- **Never smile or laugh.** Derisive or sarcastic laughter heaps
kerosene on the fire. Laughter during a disagreement can
represent the ultimate in disrespect, because it is close to
ridicule—even though you may only be laughing nervously
to ward off tension. Smile only if it's clear that you're doing
so out of loving support.

- **The neutral look works best.** This one is not easy. Even if
it makes you feel a little silly, practice a neutral demeanor in
the mirror. Neutrality puts the emphasis on the problem to
be solved and on rational thinking rather than escalating
the emotional stakes between parent and child. When we
emanate anger through our eyes, through our tones, and
through our expressions, we send a message that this is a
personal duel—a power struggle—and we will use our
parental power to win. It's a terrible mistake to let that
impression hold sway. Be gentle, emphasize the task or the
issue at hand, and respectfully let your teenager own the
responsibility for doing the right thing.

## Detonation, Delay, or Defuse

Let's review some basic insights:

1. Anger is absolutely normal and universal.
2. Anger must be confronted wisely and carefully by parents.
3. Immature people express anger unpleasantly.
4. A bit of unpleasantness now is better than a world of
   trouble later.

5. It helps to listen, be gentle and neutral, and focus on the facts.

You and your teenager are the primary characters in a little anger drama. How you handle your own emotions will make a great deal of difference. If you struggle to keep your own cool and ultimately lash out at your child, you have worsened the situation. For that reason, my first counsel to parents about handling their children's anger is to be certain they can manage their own. If your teenager is giving you problems, your own anxiety will be rising. You need to talk about it to your spouse or wise friends. Keeping a private journal is also a great idea. Write out exactly how you feel, how your relationship with your teenager is coming along, and what goals you have for the coming week in dealing with anger—yours and your child's. Make it a central part of your prayer life, trusting God to give you both wisdom and self-control. Resolve that this is a crucial rite of passage in the history of your family. You need to handle it as well as you can to help your teenager emerge as an adult of maturity and integrity.

Every one of us is potentially "explosive." We carry all those flammable chemicals within our personal constitution. During the tension of the teen years, you don't want your child's anger to detonate, wounding herself and others. You don't want it delayed so that it strikes in the form of many explosions later, and perhaps permanently. Instead, you want to defuse anger as it comes along—in bits and bites. Again, the Bible had it exactly right long before the term "passive-aggressive" was ever formulated: "Do not let the sun go down while you are still angry, and do not give the devil a foothold" (Ephesians 4:26–27). Who could express the plain truth better? Remove the anger early, before it can spread.

Settle problems and grievances in your household while they are fresh; otherwise, think of it as giving the devil a foothold.

So many problems and disputes in your family can be circumvented by keeping the channels of communication open. Keep abreast of the current events that make up your child's personal world. Be certain you're armed with the best information possible about his emotions and what may be affecting them. Be willing to help your teenager solve his problems, as long as the final goal is for him to take personal responsibility for his own actions.

I also recommend that you spend some time studying the Anger Ladder. Remember, like all ladders, it starts at the bottom and climbs upward. Adults sometimes forget the obvious: growth is a process. Young people must learn to think and act maturely, just as their parents did. The ladder concept helps because it shows us a picture of that process. It reminds us that any child must start at the bottom and climb gradually to the top. What rung represents your teenager's level of maturity? What are you doing right now to help your teenager reach for the next step?

. . . These questions bring us to our next chapter. Let's talk about your own place on that ladder.

# anger ladder

## POSITIVE

1. Pleasant • Seeking resolution • Focusing anger on source • Holding to primary complaint • Thinking logically
2. Pleasant • Focusing anger on source • Holding to primary complaint • Thinking logically

## POSITIVE AND NEGATIVE

3. Focusing anger on source • Holding to primary complaint • Thinking logically • Unpleasant, loud
4. Holding to primary complaint • Thinking logically • Unpleasant, loud • Displacing anger to other sources
5. Focusing anger on source • Holding to primary complaint • Thinking logically • Unpleasant, loud • Verbal abuse
6. Thinking logically • Unpleasant, loud • Displacing anger to other sources • Expressing unrelated complaints

## PRIMARILY NEGATIVE

7. Unpleasant, loud • Displacing anger to other sources • Expressing unrelated complaints • Emotionally destructive behavior
8. Unpleasant, loud • Displacing anger to other sources • Expressing unrelated complaints • Verbal abuse • Emotionally destructive behavior
9. Unpleasant, loud • Cursing • Displacing anger to other sources • Expressing unrelated complaints • Verbal abuse • Emotionally destructive behavior
10. Focusing anger on source • Unpleasant, loud • Cursing • Displacing anger to other sources • Throwing objects • Emotionally destructive behavior
11. Unpleasant, loud • Cursing • Displacing anger to other sources • Throwing objects • Emotionally destructive behavior

## NEGATIVE

12. Focusing anger on source • Unpleasant, loud • Cursing • Destroying property • Verbal abuse • Emotionally destructive behavior
13. Unpleasant, loud • Cursing • Displacing anger to other sources • Destroying property • Verbal abuse • Emotionally destructive behavior
14. Unpleasant, loud • Cursing • Displacing anger to other sources • Destroying property • Verbal abuse • Physical abuse • Emotionally destructive behavior
15. Passive-aggressive behavior

# keys to self-control

SIT BACK AND LISTEN SADLY TO THE TALE I'VE HEARD SO MANY times. A parent tells me, "I'm sorry, but I just can't help myself. I don't know anyone who wouldn't lose his cool if he had to cope with the behavior of my son, as I do every single day. It sure makes *me* crazy! Just a few words from that poison tongue, or that evil eye of his, and I begin to lose it. Don't you understand? It's accumulative! I put up with his sullen act for a whole weekend, and by Sunday evening I'm snapping at him and he's snapping at me. I end up yelling, slamming doors, and then he just becomes even more sullen. Dr. Campbell, it's a vicious cycle, and I don't know what to do about it."

I think you can see why this story is so disheartening. This parent has surrendered his management of the parenting responsibility. What would you say about his chances for teaching healthy anger management techniques? Have you ever heard of a piano teacher who was tone deaf? How about the leader of an Alcoholics Anonymous chapter who drank while leading the sessions? Now—you must ask yourself, *What is the effect of my self-control on my teenager's ability to maintain his own self-control?* This question is a very serious one, I know you'll agree.

> **What is the effect of my self-control on my teenager's ability to maintain his own self-control?**

The Bible offers a marvelous image of this issue: "Like a city whose walls are broken down is a man who lacks self-control" (Proverbs 25:28). David the psalmist lived during times when broken city walls were no laughing matter. Broken walls meant predatory bands of robbers and raiders were certain to show up. When we lack self-control, our own "walls" are down, for personal discipline is a protective device. But we also jeopardize those "little cities" we are building, our children. We need to help them fortify their own defenses by learning to manage their emotions.

When the apostle Paul listed the fruits of the Holy Spirit—that is, the products of spiritual maturity—he left self-control for last, for it is perhaps the most elusive of all (see Galatians 5:22–23). But it's comforting to know that this is a gift given from above. Surely those who love God and grow in their faith will see that precious fruit blossom in their lives. There are many among us who have given up trying to control their emotions. They decide it's simply genetic, as permanent as a birthmark (perhaps the mark of Cain). They understand that the worst problem of the short fuse is how short it really is. Many temptations work on us over a period of time, and we have the opportunity to consider them rationally. But when temper blows up, it happens suddenly—at least it seems that way. The words and the violence erupt almost before we can restrain them. In truth, of course, the anger has been simmering longer than we realize.

If anger is indeed an emotional issue, we can combat it with spiritual weapons, beginning with the realization that self-control comes from God and blossoms like healthy fruit. Build your faith, spend more time in prayer and reflection, and the inevitable result is a different perspective on life. Paul wrote, "Therefore, if anyone is in Christ, he is a new creation; the old has gone, the new has come!" (2 Corinthians 5:17). This doesn't mean old habits simply vanish. It does mean a *new way* is possible, through the power of God's Spirit. The task is to devote ourselves, more and more, to the new way so what the Bible calls the "old" person in us no longer limits our maturity. This means you need to have an active spiritual life, finding time to pray and study your Bible carefully. Believe me, it has everything to do with your spiritual perspective and, therefore, your ability to maintain self-control "under fire."

## Body, Mind, and Spirit

The danger, then, is in demonstrating to our children an anger we cannot overcome, even as we insist on their doing the same. That lesson is bound to fail.

I realize how difficult it is to be at our best when we're knee-deep in the trials imposed by an adolescent child. A twelve- to fifteen-year-old will display puzzling mood shifts. At just the time you think she is an impressive young lady on the verge of maturity, she will rush to her room, crying for a reason you cannot seem to ascertain. You'll notice advance and regression, and the cycle repeats: one step forward, two steps back. At least James assures us that "the testing of your faith develops perseverance" (James 1:3). You'll learn to be patient. There are times when perseverance alone will help keep you from giving in to total exasperation.

But you must give your best effort (and trust in God's strength) to keep from giving in. Here are some good reasons for doing so:

- Your uncontrolled anger will make you unapproachable to your teenager in the times she most needs you, and when she most needs to experience your loving acceptance.
- Your uncontrolled anger will cost you your teenager's respect.
- Your uncontrolled anger will send your teenager to her peers as an alternative when she need to confide in someone.

What, then, are the central requirements for self-control? You need to be healthy in body, mind, and spirit. Have you evaluated yourself against that three-point checklist lately? Though the following is basic common sense, it's good to be reminded of how best to take care of our own personal needs so that we can, in turn, better direct the needs of our family.

### Body

Many parents suffer from fatigue. Particularly in this new, turbocharged world, we try to take on the challenges of parenting while maintaining all their old interests and involvements. From early in the morning to late at night, we're expending energy. Then, with a world of issues on our minds, we have trouble sleeping. That's the setting with which we began this book.

Many parents also fail to take care of their own physical and medical needs. We may care for our children very responsibly, making every doctor and dental appointment; but our own needs take a backseat. It doesn't help that many Americans lack adequate medical insurance coverage today. A total of forty-five million lacked any coverage, according to a recent survey.[1]

Let me ask you about your caffeine dependence. I'm amazed by what I often find when I talk to parents: too many soft drinks, too much coffee. Caffeine affects different people in different ways, but never for the better when it comes to physical and emotional needs. I will add my voice to those who encourage you to depend on a healthy, low-carbohydrate breakfast with plenty of protein and bulk, and limit your caffeine intake. Don't skip breakfast or lunch. It's amazing how much better you'll feel during the afternoon if you lunch on a green salad, avoiding carbohydrates and caffeine. Then at dinner, don't overeat. This is the meal where that is most likely to happen.

**Your uncontrolled anger will cost you your teenager's respect.**

Intended as a bit of practical advice, these pointers provide you a good start in gaining self-control.

You can't be effective at any pursuit when you're tired, ill, or overstimulated. Parenting a teenager in particular is not for the weak-kneed! When was your last complete physical examination? How would you evaluate your diet and exercise? It may be hard to imagine, but simply taking a good brisk walk can sometimes help you to be a more effective parent.

## Mind

Sadly, many parents today don't realize the state of their own emotional health. You need to be at your mental and emotional best to stand up to the challenges of parenting. That means watching out for depression, fatigue, and anxiety—the chief enemies of adult emotional health. You may need to consult a specialist and get a good objective opinion on whether you're suffering from any of these. Remember, it's not just about you, but about your children and what kind of parenting they will receive. You need to be at your very best.

Give particular attention to your social balance. By that I mean your exposure to other people. Every adult has a unique social requirement. Some need more "outside" friends than others. And I've never encountered an adult who already understood that depression is strongly tied to this social equilibrium. Could it be that you spend too much time alone? Could it be that you're overly saturated with relationships, through church, PTA, neighborhood, and so on? It's important to acquire a level of control in your own life—and to understand precisely what you need emotionally—so that you can find the right balance. There are business executives who are forced to spend a great amount of time with other people, and their lack of private time makes them depressed. And, of course, there are mothers at home with four children who seldom interact with other adults, and they, too, find themselves suffering internally.

Now, considering the crucial nature of your social balance, think about the requirements of being a patient and effective parent of a teenager. No wonder so many of us have trouble controlling our emotions in parenting. The teenager will try your inner reserves, and you'll be sorely tempted to overreact emotionally—to "blow your stack."

Stack-blowing happens, particularly when we aren't mastering our own emotions. It's a fact. But if a hot temper becomes a chronic reaction on your part, there are going to be significant problems and challenges in your work as a parent. It's a powerful thing to apologize to your child when you overreact. Never let parental pride keep you from this moral necessity; it has positive value in your relationship with your teenager. You are treating her with respect. You are showing humility and remorse for your own actions, which sets a good example. And you are helping to put out some of the fires of her anger about your overreaction.

**Take care of your emotional well-being.**

But again, if you habitually lose your temper, apologies lose a significant amount of effectiveness. You might say something like, "I shouldn't yell at you like that. I shouldn't slam doors, and I'll do better." Your teenager might be thinking, *That's what you said last time.* What you're now modeling is an inability to overcome your destructive habit, and that's not the lesson any parent wants to teach.

Take care of your emotional well-being. If a doctor prescribes it, don't hesitate to use an antidepressant. There should be no stigma attached to these medications for reasons of spirituality, pride, or anything else. A diabetic wouldn't hesitate to take insulin, because it is a simple chemical requirement of his body. In the same way, we now understand that the mind has chemical requirements that may need the stimulation of an antidepressant. It just may be that even with all your personal effort to control depression, you need that prescription from your doctor.

It can make a significant difference in your performance as a parent.

## Spirit

My definition of a healthy spiritual life is one of open communication between you and God. You should periodically read and reflect on Psalm 51, in which the psalmist prays, "Create in me a pure heart, O God, and renew a steadfast spirit within me" (v. 10). Ask the Lord to search your heart and reveal to you the impurities, large and small, that hamper your spiritual life. Realize that only through the work of Christ and the daily encouragement and guidance of the Holy Spirit can you have a proper standing before God. He presents those gifts to you freely; you need only accept them. No matter how involved you become in the life of parenting, you must find personal time with God to renew that spiritual perspective and intimate blessing that only he can provide. Just as your teenager needs you to fill his or her "emotional tank" with unconditional love and acceptance, you need your own heavenly Father to do the same for you.

So spend time simply feeling and accepting God's love. Take the time to tell him about all of your adventures as a mother or father; all your trials and tribulations; all your hopes and dreams. You'll feel a great unburdening of your cares as you realize that you never walk alone—that you can feel the security and support from God that your child feels from you. At the same time, you'll realize that this same loving Lord is looking out for your teenager even when you stumble.

As for me, I often found as a parent that only when the children were in bed could I find sufficient time with God. To escape distractions, I took long walks or simply sat outdoors or in a quiet room. I understood the importance of finding the best place where God and I could be alone. Nothing can dispel your anger and give you healthy perspective like the healthy practice of taking all your cares to God.

You might take another look at the Anger Ladder at the end of Chapter 2. This time, measure yourself against it. What rung do you usually reach? How can you climb one notch higher? Making the climb is something you and your teenager can do together. From today onward, make it a central mission of your life to set your sights on the top rung—as an individual, as a parent, and as an entire family. For at that summit can be found the kind of life that brings contentment, success, and blessings for the world. That's a place we all want to be.

## More About Coping

There are other tools you can use that will provide significant help as you try to control your emotions. Let me share a few of them with you.

### Talk to Yourself

Have you ever been told that mentally healthy people don't talk to themselves? Don't believe it! Actually, self-talk can be very positive. Research has proved its connection to lowering stress, improving emotional outlook, and other positives. Self-talk simply reinforces and affirms a belief, giving it more power. It's not at all the same as generic "positive thinking"—as long as the self-talk is accurate and logical.[2] For example, you can tell yourself, "I can throw a fastball 100 miles per hour," and it won't help you at all if you don't have that ability—particularly if you *know* you don't have that ability. But each of us has considerable ability to regulate our emotions. When you use self-talk to affirm to yourself that you can set a good example of anger management, you've taken a positive step.

Whether we realize it or not, we all use self-talk. How often has some thought like the following moved through your mind: *I have no willpower. I know I won't resist that second helping of ice cream.* In this instance, self-talk reinforces negative behavior patterns. The statement at the beginning of this chapter, uttered by the frustrated parent, is an example of "captured" self-talk shared with a listener. The parent tells himself that he's not capable of doing any better, and he creates a very tragic self-fulfilling prophecy.

> **When you listen to what God says about you, and reinforce it through self-talk, you provide your own encouragement to be strong.**

But when you listen to what God says about you, and reinforce it through self-talk, you provide your own encouragement to be strong. For example, you can commit this verse to memory: "For we are God's workmanship, created in Christ Jesus to do good works, which God prepared in advance for us to do" (Ephesians 2:10). The word *workmanship* carried the original meaning of a masterpiece, as in the greatest work of art. That's how God sees you. Knowing that makes you realize you *can* control yourself. You need not give way to anger.

In my own experience as a parent, I used certain thoughts repeatedly because they worked for me. For example, I would tell myself, "If it's the last thing I do, I'm not going to let my teenager make me angry! I know I'm stronger than he is, and I can hold my anger in if I set my mind to it. The bottom line is that I love my child, and my love is bigger than this one headache." Just dwelling on that thought gave me a dose of truth, and I found I could control my temper.

Another example I put to frequent use was: "I recognize this behavior. My child is bringing his anger to me, where I can help him deal with it. I know that's a whole lot better than if he took it somewhere to the outside world or turned it into a destructive direction. And it's better for me to deal with it now than see it again later as stealth anger." Again, I was simply recognizing reality—claiming the perspective that put everything in its proper space and helped me take charge of the situation in a positive way.

Use self-talk not only "on the spot," but at other times as you reflect on your parenting skills. It's a way of rehearsing the right solutions so the wrong ones won't become entrenched.

## Talk to Others

The traditional kind of talk can be helpful too. Every single one of us needs the support and encouragement of like-minded adults. This is why Sunday morning Bible study classes and other groups can be very helpful to parents—and why you definitely shouldn't say that you no longer have time for them. It's very natural in the cycle of an adult's life to socialize much less once the spouse and the children enter the picture. Family becomes the essence of our life—and that in itself is healthy and good. But in "cocooning" with family, we find ourselves too cut off from others. As John Donne put it, no man (or woman) is an island. As parents, we need our friends more than ever. So I urge you to find other parents and share your burdens together.

You might consider starting a parenting support group with friends who are also raising teenagers. Imagine how much your burden would be eased by sharing the questions of your family life with like-minded friends. You would give and receive support in a way that is healthy and refreshing.

Finally, as obvious as it sounds, talk to your spouse. Support each other. When raising teenagers, parents need to be on the same page. They need to carefully communicate what their stances and decisions will be so that a teenager cannot cause friction by playing them against each other. Who else in the world knows both you and your teenager better than your spouse?

## "Talk" to a Journal

You can also talk with a pen or a computer, can't you? Many parents find journaling to be a very useful outlet. It's another way of disciplining yourself to be reflective. As you sit down and record your emotions and their effects on your behavior during the day, you'll gain new insights about yourself just by committing these things to paper. Journaling works very well with prayer life, by the way. You can combine the two in an activity that will empower you to grow emotionally and set a great example for your teenager.

There's a very interesting thought in Psalm 4:4: "In your anger do not sin; when you are on your beds, search your hearts and be silent." Notice first that anger is not the same as sin, but a possible stimulus to sin. In the New Testament, James tells us the same thing about temptation (see James 1:14–15). Sin comes when we let these impulses affect our behavior. The psalmist assumes that we will be angry, but counsels us to retire to our rest, keep silence, and search our hearts. This is the source of the old admonition to avoid letting the sun set on our anger—and the corollary that "he who goes to sleep in anger shares his bed with the devil" (see Ephesians 4:26–27). The point is that we should reflect deeply upon our emotions, ideally with the help of a journal and prayer. Then the devil gets no foothold and the anger is defused.

## Talk to God

It's worth saying again. You are loved and supported by the greatest Parent there could ever be. Remember the incredible promise found in Philippians 4:6–7: "Do not be anxious about anything, but in everything, by prayer and petition, with thanksgiving, present your requests to God. And the peace of God, which transcends all understanding, will guard your hearts and your minds in Christ Jesus." It's wonderful, and it's true. The final fruit of the Spirit is self-control, and it comes to all those who love Christ and follow him until his ways become their ways; until his desires become their desires; and until his love, grace, and mercy begin to cast out the shadows of life—even those of an angry and rebellious teenager.

## A Model of Forgiveness

Finally, as you look at your own emotions and behavior, consider the essential place of forgiveness. I've often said that forgiveness is giving up the right to get even. Bitterness is a destructive cancer within us. It is anger that is entrenched. Your teenager needs to learn that bitterness is enslavement, while forgiveness is liberation. The best way you can teach him is to present a model of it in your own behavior.

One would imagine that forgiveness of one's own child would

come naturally, but of course it does not. It's heartbreaking to find parents who have no mercy for their own offspring. It's worth reflecting on how you would respond if your child committed some terrible act. Is there any line beyond which you could not forgive your child? Is there any line beyond which God would not forgive you? As God has been merciful to each of us, we must do the same. That's our biblical imperative as believers. Your teenager is surely going to stumble occasionally in his behavior. We hope and pray it won't be in any devastating way. But when she does,

> **Forgiveness is giving up the right to get even.**

she needs a reaffirmation of your unconditional love—a model of God's mercy and grace expressed through you. When she sees that your love is all-encompassing—and greater than her successes and failures—then she will know she can come to you for training. She can bring any problem to you. Conversely, if she feels there are actions for which she has not been forgiven, then she will begin to take her problems and needs elsewhere.

You need to accept your teenager's forgiveness. Are there not times when we, the parents, are the ones who stumble? Don't we occasionally raise our voices when we shouldn't or say demeaning words that we regret? We are imperfect, and therefore missteps are inevitable. When they occur, we should not be too proud to approach our children to ask forgiveness. Consider what happens when we do this. We are granting respect and dignity to our teenagers. This is an invaluable treasure to a teenager. We are presenting a model of humility and repentance rather than of pride and arrogance—a model they can follow. We are highlighting the teenager's need to forgive as well as our human need to receive mercy. We are cutting off anger (in each of us) before it has the chance to put down roots.

In short, there are many wonderful things that transpire spiritually, mentally, and emotionally when grace is given and received between parent and child. Mercy and forgiveness are powerful spiritual forces that break the cycle of sin and retribution in this world. The connection between us grows ever stronger and more resonant when we reach out to one another in our brokenness.

You also need to model forgiveness in other relationships; for example, forgiveness of your spouse and of those outside your home. Please know that if there is "unfinished business" between you and your marriage partner, it affects your children as much as yourselves. Among other things, it gives them a negative view of marriage that may prevent them from starting families. Concerning those outside your home, watch how you speak about your boss, your coworkers, your pastor and fellow church members, your neighbors, and others. One pastor said that he knew what the adults were saying about him by looking into the eyes of their children. Measure your social behavior against Paul's checklist, knowing that your teenager will watch you carefully:

Love is patient, love is kind. It does not envy, it does not boast, it is not proud. It is not rude, it is not self-seeking, it is not easily angered, it keeps no record of wrongs. Love does not delight in evil but rejoices with the truth. It always protects, always trusts, always hopes, always perseveres. (1 Corinthians 13:4–7)

Anger is almost the most powerful force there is. *Almost.* There are a few powers that are even greater: love, grace, and mercy, for

**Anger is overcome by the love of God.**

example. God graciously lavishes these powers upon us, and that allows us to lavish them upon our spouses, upon our children, and upon everyone who becomes a supporting character in the drama of our lives. Even as we attempt to control our own emotions and train our children to do the same, we should remember that anger is overcome by the love of God. That solid truth should have the greatest possible impact on our performance as parents. Our heavenly Father, you see, sets the ultimate example for managing anger:

> For his anger lasts only a moment,
>     but his favor lasts a lifetime;
> weeping may remain for a night,
>     but rejoicing comes in the morning. (Psalm 30:5)

What a wonderful way to look at anger. Even God experiences it. As we said at the beginning of the second chapter, anger is a *good* thing. If we hold on to it too long, it becomes something harmful and damaging. But if we handle it briefly and manage it effectively—the work of "only a moment" for God—we transform its energy into something useful. Thus, as the psalmist says, weeping can turn to rejoicing. And if you can master that skill, and teach your teenager to do the same, you will have in your hands the key to a healthy and happy life.

# 4

# love: the essential solution

LET ME ASK YOU TWO QUESTIONS:

1. When you were a child, did your parents love you?
2. Did you feel sincerely loved at the time?

Here is an enigma to ponder. I have never met a parent who didn't love his or her children. And yet I have met countless men, women, and children who did not feel loved by their parents.

How can those two points both be true? What happens to love on its way from the parent to the child? Does it vanish in the air somehow?

Many of us reach mature adulthood before we realize, after great reflection, that our parents did indeed love us. *They just weren't good at showing it.* If you did feel thoroughly and unconditionally

If you felt thoroughly and unconditionally loved as a child, then the chances are you are a healthy and well-balanced adult.

loved, then the chances are you are a healthy and well-balanced adult.

This is a profoundly important point, fellow parent. If anger is your greatest enemy; if indeed it is the wolf at the door of your home—then what is the greatest power available to you? Love, of course. But it isn't enough to simply feel love for our children. No matter what the popular conception may be, when we love another person that person doesn't "just know." They don't know we love them simply because we say the words. Even providing food, clothing, and shelter isn't enough to get the message across. So how do our children know we love them? Through our actions.

John, the disciple of Jesus, wrote these words: "This is how we know what love is: Jesus Christ laid down his life for us. And we ought to lay down our lives for our brothers . . . Dear children, let us not love with words or tongue but with actions and in truth" (1 John 3:16, 18).

What are the key words here? *Actions; truth; laid down his life.* These words suggest that we must do all we can to make our love real, giving all that we have and all that we are. It is so crucial, because a child who feels unconditionally loved has a solid foundation from which to build a happy and successful life. But a child who lacks that essential understanding will become more and more angry, for love is what every human being—particularly every child—needs and craves the most.

In a way, Jesus had twelve unruly children—all of them boys!

The Bible tells us that when he prepared to leave them to face the world on their own, he related to them very carefully and intentionally.

It was just before the Passover Feast. Jesus knew that the time had come for him to leave this world and go to the Father. Having loved his own who were in the world, he now showed them the full extent of his love. (John 13:1)

Other translations render that last phrase to say that he loved them "to the last." He gave them all he had, he showed it in action (the foot washing immediately followed) as well as teaching, and he taught about one topic more than any other: love.

You have loved "your own" from the beginning, and you intend to love them to the last, showing the full extent of your love. When your children were little, you said those three words all the time: *I love you.* What you may not have realized is that adults learn *verbally,* but children learn *visually* and *experientially.* This means when we used that beautiful word, it had a complex wealth of associations for us (and for other adults) that our children didn't share. To them it was a simple word, synonymous with "like." Their young hearts craved love, but hearing the words didn't fill their need. This is the reason your young child sought your attention in various ways. Attention far more than words communicated love. Time and interaction communicated love. Only as your children became older did they begin to understand abstract ideas such as the idea of love.

I heard the story of a man who fell in love. He was eloquent and expressive with words, so he began to write the young lady a new letter every day. Each letter included a new poem about his love for her. Each day he found new ways to describe his over-powering affection. He described his love in every manner and metaphor one might conceive. But somehow he just wasn't breaking through. So the young man stepped up his efforts. He began to write her twice a day. Finally, he was writing her a new letter every four of his waking hours. And what came out of it? The young lady married the mailman.

I suppose it had never occurred to that young man that love comes experientially, not verbally. It certainly does for children, but it's true also for teenagers. Even at their stage of maturity, teenagers need powerful and consistent demonstrations that they are unconditionally loved. Attention, time, and interaction still communicate love more powerfully than words. But wait, don't our teenagers push us away at times? Yes, they do. Again, theirs is largely a subconscious need. Most teenagers could not articulate what they truly feel or want. They are restless, they want something, they need something, but they probably don't realize they need precisely the same thing they needed as little children. They need regular and significant expressions of our love.

They need it even as they mutate—mind, soul, and body—to some new kind of person; even as they stumble through puberty, develop acne, and feel ugly and awkward. They seek outside friendship, of course. They struggle in that pursuit, because their friends are experiencing the same tensions. It's tough to live through these years, and teenagers need to know, more firmly than ever, that their parents still adore them. They need to be certain that no matter how much they grow,

**Your parental love is your teenager's rock and shelter.**

change, and struggle with their emotions, that love will hold firm. No matter how difficult it may be understand your teenager, your parental love is his rock and his shelter. Therefore, leave no question in his mind about the state of your commitment.

Easier said than done, of course. How can we lay down our lives, in action and in truth, to prove our love for our children?

## Bobby's Story

Bobby was the last fellow you'd have expected to get into trouble. But now he was getting into trouble frequently. He had made good grades through elementary school and the first part of high school. He was sharp, attractive, and popular with his friends. He was a good athlete—a pitcher in baseball, a quarterback in football, and a shooting guard in basketball. He played soccer and tennis during whatever time was left over. He was just the type of boy that made other parents whisper among themselves, "Why can't our child be more like Bobby?"

But sometime around the age of fifteen, Bobby's world became shrouded by dark clouds. His grades dropped. He stopped caring about his appearance and his friends. He developed a very sarcastic demeanor. Then came the shoplifting problem. Why would the son of a well-to-do family shoplift? He had everything he wanted or needed. For that matter, his parents had been lavishing gifts upon him as his life spun more out of control. They thought perhaps he would appreciate those gifts and start "cleaning up his act."

What became noticeable about Bobby was that he kept returning to the subject of sports. He didn't even realize how often that topic wandered back into his conversation. Bobby had loved his games. He had been good in every one of them, and it had pleased his father so much. Dad coached some of the Little League teams, came to every game, made hours of home video film. Even Mom was the devoted team mother. And therein lay the problem, as it became clear.

Bobby had come to feel that all his worth as a son came from achievement on the playing field. If he could hit more baskets, if he could throw more touchdown passes, if he could log more strikeouts—well, it just seemed those were the times his parents showed their love. If he had a big game, the family got to go out for pizza, his favorite. Bobby saw old pictures of himself as a baby, with an oversized baseball cap drooping over his eyes. His purpose in life was to excel in athletics. At least that's how it seemed to him. And the day came when he wondered what would happen if he got tired of baseball, football, basketball, and the rest. What if he got hurt and couldn't play? What if some other kid was better?

Bobby began making hints about dropping a sport or two. Maybe he could use the time for something else. But whenever he suggested such a possibility, his parents became alarmed. "But you love that game!" "You've invested so much time in being the best—how could you drop that sport?" Or, "I know you're not serious. You're too smart to give up something you're so good at."

Bobby felt as if there were some unwritten sports contract between him and his parents. All of their time together had always revolved around practices, games, or shooting baskets together in the backyard. He felt trapped—and angry about it.

The truth was that Bobby's parents loved him very much, with or without athletics. But somehow they had forgotten they needed to show it clearly. The whole sports thing had just *evolved* as Bobby came along in life. If they had understood what was at stake, they would have happily said good-bye to sports for good and simply enjoyed their son.

Their greatest need was to show that their love was unconditional, that it had no "ifs" attached, and that it didn't come and go. When Bobby dropped his hints, he was actually asking his parents, "Do you love me?" He had no way of knowing what would happen if sports were removed from the picture. The answer may have seemed obvious to any parent, but it wasn't to a fifteen-year-old.

## Love Without Strings

True love, the kind that exists between parent and child, must be *unconditional.* I expect that you're aware of the meaning of that term, but let's take a moment to qualify exactly what it means.

Unconditional love has no strings attached; it is not a contract that must be fulfilled, but a commitment without qualification. When your teenager brings home a poor grade, you're not happy about the grade. But you still love your teenager. When he acts insolent, you don't love his behavior. But he should be certain that your love for him is not affected. If you have established a deep mutual relationship of unconditional love, there will never be a time when he cannot come to you with a serious problem. Your teenager will be confident and secure, because he will have reached this point in his life from a working foundation of your unshakable acceptance and support.

In other words, you have to make it clear in your home that though there is good and bad behavior, love is not on the table for negotiation. It cannot be revoked. It is something like that precious heirloom wedding ring your great-grandmother wore, which you keep in the safest possible place. (You might show your teenager something like that as an illustration, as you describe your unconditional love.)

Most parents feel that they love their children unconditionally. The problem is, they unintentionally communicate that when the teenager's actions are displeasing, love may be withheld. My wife, Pat, and I raised three kids through the teenage years. We made a covenant between ourselves that we would hold to the highest ideal, the biblical ideal of love for our children. That ideal can be found in Romans 8:38–39:

> For I am convinced that neither death nor life, neither angels nor demons, neither the present nor the future, nor any powers, neither height nor depth, nor anything else in all creation, will be able to separate us from the love of God that is in Christ Jesus our Lord.

In this passage the apostle Paul does his eloquent best to leave no question that God's love for us through Christ is an absolute. God has taken the initiative. His love has absolutely nothing to do with our worthiness. He simply loves us because we are his children. And nothing in creation can tear us from his embrace. End of story.

This is the very model for how we are to love our *own* children (as well as others). We are to love proactively in a way that has nothing to do with the behavior of our children. Pat and I knew there would be times when the behavior itself would test us. But there would never be a chance of our losing even an ounce of our love for our children. So the problem was in being sure they understood that perfectly. As parents, we made it a point to silently and regularly remind ourselves:

- Teenagers are still children.
- Children are emotionally immature.
- Emotionally immature behavior is unpleasant.
- If my love seems lessened by such behavior, my children will not feel loved.
- Unfelt love leads to insecurity, poor self-image, and many worse things.
- Unconditional love makes my children strong, confident, secure, and healthy.

Ask yourself this question: *Although my children probably* know *they are loved, do they* feel *it?*

Debbie was a fifteen-year-old who didn't feel it. Her parents, who loved her very much, never would have guessed. But after a sharp downturn in the events of her life, they were growing desperate. She had seemingly lost interest in nearly every facet of her life. She had been a fine student, but now she struggled to pass her classes. She no longer cared about friends, church, clothing, music, or her once-favorite television shows. She was listless and spoke in grunts and "uh-huhs." After a while, however, she began to be more transparent in our sessions together. It was very clear that she felt no one in the world cared about her, and she cared for no one.

> Unconditional love makes my children strong, confident, secure, and healthy.

Her parents had been the type who celebrated achievements and good grades. But when even minor disappointments came, they were . . . well, just disappointed. They often told her she could do better. They offered rewards for successes, and—as things began to slide—penalties for poor performance. At age thirteen, ingrained within Debbie was the idea that she was loved only when she achieved every desirable goal. Whatever her parents might actually say, their actions communicated a clear message to her. Because Debbie, like all young people, had a powerful need for love, she felt powerful pressure. As she struggled, she felt unloved and unable to love others—parents or friends.

As with many cases I've witnessed, this story fortunately had a happy ending. Debbie and her parents needed to understand the genuine dynamics of their family problem. The parents had to learn to clearly express unconditional love for their daughter. And when that happened, all aspects of her life gradually began to improve.

*That's all well and good,* you may be thinking, *but what I'm looking for are* specific actions *I can take to make unconditional love an undeniable reality in the emotional atmosphere of my home.* Hang on—I'll give you a clear concept of what must be done, then I'll give you three ways to do it.

## Filling the Tank

The foundational idea I have taught is this: teenagers need a consistent feeling of unconditional love from their parents. The word picture I have used for clarification is that of a tank that might require fuel. Your teenager needs love in the same way your car needs gasoline. Your car needs to be filled regularly, and if you let the fuel gauge show "empty," your car will be halted in its tracks. It won't move another foot.

In the same way, you need to keep your teenager's emotional

tank filled. You can't expect that expressing your love once, or even a few times, will be enough. That "fuel" will work itself through your teenager's system, providing strength and assurance, then it will be gone. This is simply a universal fact of human nature. The truth is that when your teenager has a full tank—when he is certain of an unconditional love that his parents feel for him—he can live as effectively as a good car can drive. He will function well in his world, and he will be capable of learning and growth. A child of any age will constantly be asking, "Do you love me?" through his actions.

But if he is not receiving the answer he needs, he will feel unloved. Then the consequences will be very negative, and they will be seen in his behavior. Why does a little one often misbehave? Any parent knows that the child is "looking for attention." That's another way of saying the child is asking, "Do you love me?" The more the parent supplies the answer, through his or her own actions, the less misbehavior there will be. If you want proof of this principle, watch a three-year-old in public sometime—for example, sitting in church with his parents. The child will assert his independence by investigating what's on the floor, by peering at the neighbors in the next pew, or by some other activity. Then, at a certain point, the child will turn back to the parent for eye contact, physical touch, or focused attention. These assure the child he has not been forgotten in the midst of this church service. If the parent refuses to quietly attend to that empty tank, the result will be increased disruptiveness.

Teenagers may not make it quite so obvious as younger children will. But they are still children, they ask the same basic question, and they need the same assurance. And with their broader reach into the world—school, friends, and so on—they are able to act out their frustration in ways that are much more harmful. A teenager understands subconsciously that a drop in grades is a certain way to get some quick attention, because most parents are very interested in their child's grades. Physical appearance, increased volume on the stereo, refusal to attend church with the family—these may, in some circumstances, represent a child's trying to engage the full attention of his parents. This isn't to say that if you love your child adequately, he will conform to all of your desires for his appearance, activities, and so forth. But he will not be actively looking for new avenues to express anger or frustration.

**A teenager is like a mirror; she reflects what she is given.**

In a way, a teenager is like a mirror; she reflects what she is given. If you pour love and affection into your teenager, she will be capable of showing love and affection to you, to those around her, and eventually to a life mate and children. But if she doesn't feel loved and accepted, she will have no love and acceptance to give. Like anything else, love is learned. You may have noticed that many parents have trouble expressing affection to their children or to anyone because their own parents didn't express it to them. In Bobby's case (his story appears earlier in this chapter), if we didn't identify the problem and correct it, he would grow into an adult who works hard but never feels that his work is enough. And his own approval would always come with a price.

Do you remember the character of Ebenezer Scrooge in Dickens's *A Christmas Carol*? We discover in the story that when he was a boy, his father sent him away to school and withheld affection, still angry that his wife had died in childbirth. Young Ebenezer received love from his sister, but that wasn't enough. He craved a parental love he never received. The result, of course, was that he became a bitter, unloving man who worked hard and had no idea how to express affection. There is a great deal of truth in that character.

All those problems are solved when you simply keep the emotional tank full. It isn't so difficult—just express the love you already have. It would be a challenge to list all the things that go better in your home when your teenager's love requirement has been met. Channels of communication between you are much more open. The teenager who feels your love is far less likely to shut you out. As I've mentioned, grades are likely to be better. Obedience is likely to improve. Your teenager will pursue his gifts and talents more effectively and eagerly. Such contemporarily common problems as depression and substance abuse are far less likely. And beyond any doubt, your teenager will come to you ready to be trained when he feels loved.

The key to unconditional love, then, is filling the emotional tank. It must be constantly refilled. But what are those three ways of filling it? I mentioned them above: focused attention, eye contact, and physical touch. Let's explore each of these in the next chapter.

# 5

## three ways to show love

### Focused Attention

Every one of us leads a busy life filled with tasks and responsibilities. Sometimes we tend to pay attention to what is temporarily demanding rather than what is ultimately important. How many times a day does this happen without our realizing it? Your teenager is needing some of your time and is sending signals accordingly—even overtly seeking a discussion. But it will have to wait, because you're looking for some important tax information. At this very moment, it seems as if there is nothing in the world more important than that document. But beneath the surface of your events, what could be more important than your teenager's emotional needs? What could have greater implications for his future?

This is a tough one. There are simply times when you have to stop and attend to practical matters: tax information, a lost set of car keys, frozen groceries that need to be put away. For that matter, there are also times when you simply need a few private moments of your own, to read a book or to watch a television show. It's hard to ascertain where the line is drawn—to know which are key moments for your teenager. What is more certain is that your teenager has a tremendous need for focused attention.

**The time you spend with your teenager can become a powerful expression of your love.**

That means a time completely devoted to him and his world. It takes personal discipline to create those times, because you and your teenager are moving in different directions all the time. But once you realize how important this principle is, I believe you'll make it a point to find that time. We all find the time to do the things we set as top priority. So it's simply a matter of truly believing that if you fail to give focused attention to your teenager, the consequences in his life will be negative and far-reaching.

Notice that the other two strategies, eye contact and physical touch, can be incorporated into this one. That's why it's so irreplaceable. The time you spend with your teenager can become a powerful expression of your love. It can build your relationship and mutual understanding like nothing else. Imagine the time a boy spends with his father, hunting or fishing. Even though they're both giving their attention to an activity, they've found a good way to spend focused time together. As they fish, the father can be careful to keep good eye contact. He can find occasion to place an affirming hand on his son's shoulder and express love through other kinds of physical touch. Fishing is long and leisurely, so good, unhurried conversations are likely to occur.

But fishing is only one example of what you can do to draw closer to your teenager. In my own experiences as a parent, I discovered that there are some real knacks to making this work in your home. I'd like to offer you some of those secrets.

## Be Intentional

You must take the initiative and select your target times. For example, when my daughter, Carey, took music lessons, I made it a tradition for me to pick her up afterward. Then we went out for a meal together. We were away from home, so there were no interruptions. We were doing something Carey enjoyed. I'm sure you can find a regular and effective setting for spending time with your teenager.

## Be Patient

Teenagers are typically reserved, and it takes a certain period of time for them to become ready to talk seriously. I picked a restaurant with slow service, and we took our time ordering. This gave Carey time to "warm up" to transparent sharing. In the meantime we casually discussed more superficial subjects. I had the opportunity to show I was interested in the little things about her life as well as the big ones. Focused time can't be a clock-watching activity to check off your list. To work well, it must be sincere and truly devoted. It's also true that as your child's age increases, the time you spend will have to increase with it.

## Provide an Escape Hatch

By the time Carey was really sharing her heart with me, we were in the car and on our way home. I understood that this was good timing, because when the conversation became a bit "heavy" or difficult to discuss, my daughter knew she would soon be able to pop out of the car, bound into the house, and take up something else. Your child will never truly open up with you if there is a fear of losing some kind of freedom. The teenager must be able to initiate the subjects she wants to discuss, then break it off when she wants. That brings us to the next principle.

## Be Approachable

Being intentional and setting the time is great strategy. But you also need to let your teenager come to you at times. This makes two requirements of you: (1) that you keep yourself open for discussion—a true discipline, and (2) that you understand the subtle signals. Carey established the following method for letting us know she needed to talk. She came into the bedroom when Pat and I were reading, preparing for sleep. (Your teenager will be aware of the quietest, most approachable times.) Her pretense was to borrow some item from the bathroom. Then, on the way out the door, she would say, "By the way . . ." Many significant conversations were opened with "By the way." She would sit at the foot of our bed after a few moments, quietly talking with us. Sooner or later she would be lying across the foot of the bed, relaxed and transparent. I remember my tendency to say something like, "Be sure you turn off the hall light

> **Be approachable and be alert for your teenager's signals.**

on the way out." Pat would kick me beneath the covers to let me know that was exactly the wrong thing to say. Be approachable and be alert for your teenager's signals.

## Be Attentive

I'm certain you know that you need to be a good listener. It's amazing how few good listeners we encounter in the world today. Can you listen to a complete sentence or thought without jumping in to make an observation of your own? Your teenager will often want to know your advice, and you'll know when that's true. But many other times your teenager will simply want you to listen. He'll want you know what it feels like in his world. It may take true self-restraint for you to avoid sharing all the information you have at every moment. You may not need to share that story from your own adolescence. You have to be discerning, but err on the side of listening sympathetically.

## Be Empathetic

Empathy is the ability to "walk a mile in someone else's shoes." Make it a point to put yourself in your teenager's place and ask yourself, *How does it feel to be in his position?* You need to understand the world of teenagers. It doesn't function at all like the world of adults—compare your own life experiences and you'll realize this is true. For example, teenage society is sorted out based on popularity and acceptance. There are various groups and cliques to fit into, and there is always a "pecking order," as with chickens. Teenagers are constantly agonizing over this pecking order. What kind of designer clothing do they need? What kind of music are they supposed to like? You will find it all superficial, but this is the world your teenager lives in, and you must accept it as a starting point for discussion.

Understanding that world will be one more reminder of why your teenager has such a great need for unconditional love at home. Adolescent society can be very unloving, very demanding, very rejecting. Because of the pecking order, teenagers tend to relate to others via guilt and envy. That is, they envy those they perceive to be "above" them; they feel guilty about those who seem "below." Listen for the power of guilt and envy as your teenager expresses his observations and emotions about others.

Focused attention, armed with this kind of clear understanding, will give you every opportunity to help teach and train your teenager. You can gently but consistently help him see biblical values in the midst of superficial adolescent values. You can demonstrate again and again that envy isn't necessary because God makes each one of us unique and special. You can show that guilt is equally inapplicable because God gives us opportunities to serve and to love everyone we know.

Focused attention will make all the difference in your teenager's transition years. All the building blocks of a happy, healthy, and successful adulthood can be laid during this time.

## Eye Contact

Imagine yourself at a high-school class reunion. The room is large, crowded, and filled with laughter and reminiscing. You tap the shoulder of an old friend whom you haven't seen in years. As you eagerly begin to talk to him, his eyes briefly find yours, then seem to wander somewhere over your shoulder, to the far end of the room. As you continue your discourse, hoping to spark a good conversation, your friend's eyes are always scanning the room.

When a conversational partner has "roving eyes," what do you conclude? How do you feel about this person? How does the person make you feel about yourself?

Every human being instinctively understands the basic and significant information transmitted through the "windows of the soul." Recent research indicates that we begin to interpret eye contact as early as forty-eight hours after birth.[1] Throughout life, a wide range of nonverbal communication transpires between us based simply on what happens when our eyes meet—or don't meet, as the case may be. Scientific studies show an ever-increasing role for eye contact in our relationships and communication. It is one significant trait (along with the presence of speech, music, and human touch, for example) that researchers insist will actually affect the physiological development of the brain—that is, the quality of the wiring between cells. During key growth periods of the human mind—and we now understand that adolescence is one of those—that "wiring" will have a tremendous impact on mental development.[2]

We seldom realize just how much information goes back and forth through the eyes. And most of that information is emotional. Eyes can be used to communicate anger, threat, fear, love, and nearly any other emotion. When we are lecturing, we "stare them down." Therefore, eye contact alone isn't necessarily a positive thing. But through the pupil and iris we have a powerful opportunity to express loving acceptance and understanding in a way words cannot express. At the same time, when our minds are somewhere else, our eyes will tell the tale. Your teenager will look into them deeply, just as he will listen to tone of voice and observe your body language.

Every parent needs to be frequently reminded about the power of the eyes. On those occasions when you're talking to your teenager, use your whole face to show your love and interest. Turn the television off or put your magazine down if they keep attracting your gaze. Keep a comfortable, nonstaring eye contact, allowing your teenager to look away when he becomes uncomfortable. Smile, nod, and demonstrate your comprehension when appropriate. "Active listening" skills can be helpful too. This refers to reflecting back a thought or emotion of what your teenager has said, clarifying what you've heard, and showing your attention: "So you're feeling a little tired of the way your friend is acting?" Don't forget that in the process you're modeling good communication skills to your teenager. I have found through my counseling that many adolescents simply haven't been taught to look someone in the eye when addressing them. Teenagers with poor self-esteem often haven't considered what they communicate about themselves through their body language.

Sometimes it's difficult to have good eye contact with a teenager. He seems intent on not meeting your gaze. He answers in grunts and tries to wander away. He resists your attempts to meet him where he is emotionally. On such occasions, don't make the mistake of forcing the issue. No one likes to be plied with questions when he isn't in the mood. Perhaps the best message you can send at the time is one of availability. You respect his feelings, and it's okay if he doesn't feel like talking. The doors are open, and when he's ready to talk, you will be too. If you become insistent, you can damage the trust in your relationship, and you can make your teenager feel

> **One of the most difficult tasks for a parent is knowing when to retreat.**

intimidated and powerless. One of the most difficult tasks for a parent is knowing when to retreat.

## Physical Touch

Research has shown that newborn babies absolutely require physical touch by nurturing adults. Otherwise, their cognitive development can be severely damaged. Certain important brain chemicals are released in the child when she is touched. Premature infants who were massaged for fifteen minutes three times a day gained weight 47 percent faster than others who were left alone in their incubators—and they were visibly more active.[3]

The fact is, those infants will continue to need the stimulation of physical contact as growing children, teenagers, young adults, and elderly citizens. This is a basic human need. Consider your own years of development. Did your parents touch or embrace you often? How did you feel about it? We all learn from our own parents, and many parents fail to provide sufficient physical touch because their own parents failed in that area. This is particularly true for the American male. For generations we have glorified the image of the "rugged individual"—the Marlboro man who roams the prairie and needs no one else. We raise our sons with TV shows and movies

> **The stimulation of physical contact is a basic human need.**

that tell them a hero is someone like Clint Eastwood who is quicker with his fists than his feelings. Many fathers and sons feel awkward about touching in any way other than a firm handshake and perhaps an occasional pat on the shoulder.

In general, the relationship between parent and child undergoes a difficult transition at the stage of adolescence. You may have touched your younger child much more frequently—hugging him, placing him in your lap, and giving him a kiss on the cheek. Fathers will carry their little children for "shoulder rides" and play with them much more physically. But they're less certain how to relate to this no-longer-child, not-quite-adult figure the child has become.

Sometimes parents compensate by giving their teenage children gifts and privileges. They intend to demonstrate their affection, but the message is far less clear than it might be through focused attention, eye contact, and physical touch. As a matter of fact, many parents today become far too permissive in what they allow their children to do and where they allow them to go. This permissiveness may spring from social pressure or simply confusion about how to show love and affection to a teenager.

Your teenager will be glad to receive the gift, but his deepest need is your authentic and regular expression of unconditional love. And though it may be more difficult now, you must find the right occasions for gentle and loving physical contact. There are times when your teenager may cut you off from eye contact, yet you can still walk up and touch the shoulder or neck. You need not make a great event of it; simply offer the casual pat as you pass by on your way to another room. He is unlikely to shrink away from such a gesture, and your message is certain to come through. It says, "We're not even talking or interacting right now. We need nothing in particular from each other at this moment, but I just want you to know I think you're great."

He's unlikely to show any vivid reaction. But he knows. And the best part is that there are many good opportunities for this type of contact. The gentle and loving touch is more casual and less intense than eye contact. It is a regular priming of the pump of your relationship. It's also something that continues to work a little while after a more unpleasant episode. Perhaps you've just said no to a request or reprimanded him for misbehavior. Again, the casual touch can smother the sparks of anger before they begin their slow ignition. Think of focused attention as the full meal, eye contact as good nutrition, and physical touch as a healthy snack.

Imagine a setting in which your son has been upset or withdrawn. Focused attention of any considerable amount isn't possible for the time being; eye contact isn't going to happen. But you walk by your son's room, find an excuse to knock on the door (if it is closed), and hand him some belonging. You stand for a second, casually observing the room, and pick some item of significance—let's say a sporting trophy. (All of this assumes, of course, that he is not too upset for you to enter his sanctuary.) You sit beside him on the bed and ask him a question about the occasion when he won the trophy. All of this is done casually, unhurriedly. But you're sitting side by side, your legs are touching, and you reminisce together about a positive past event. It's a wonderful way to keep a loving connection and switch the focus to a subject that underlines your positive relationship.

Back-scratching was a favorite of my children. Pat and I took advantage of the opportunity to apply some physical touch. Back-scratching has an amazing effect in lowering someone's defenses. When my son, David, returned from a week away at camp, I noticed that he made two requests: talk and read with him and scratch his back. David didn't realize it, but he was pulling up to the emotional service station and asking us to "fill 'er up!" I know of few better ways to fill the emotional tank than through loving physical contact.

What about embracing or a kiss on the cheek? Yes, there are times when you'll find this to be appropriate. As you can imagine, it would be a big mistake to go to the well too often in this category. Teenagers can feel awkward about "messy displays." But when he leaves for a trip and when he comes home, take advantage of the opportunity to show your love. When he wins an award or reaches some milestone, he'll be open to this level of affection.

On the other hand, you will find that when your teenager comes to you in emotional pain, her head down and sorrow written across her face, you can fill her tank with a parental hug. She has come to you because she is hurting, and she needs you to demonstrate that you love her unconditionally, including such a time as when she is unhappy and not at her best.

Then there are occasions that fit into none of the above scenarios—your teenager needs a hug *just because.* The reason is not as important as the immediate necessity. Just take advantage of one more opportunity to fill the emotional tank. You have to pick your times carefully.

Finally, here is a question parents love to ask me: "My child hasn't been receiving enough physical touch or eye contact," they say. "I can see that now. So how can I make up for it?"

That's a good question. Don't put down this book, run to your teenager, and overcompensate. He'll think you've lost your mind! These are devices that must be used in the right amount and at the right time. Instead of trying to play catch-up, simply observe your teenager and decide what the right amounts are and when the right times are. Then begin to use eye contact and offer physical touch whenever you get a chance until it becomes a strong part of your relationship.

When the time comes that you apply all three relationship-builders effectively—eye contact, physical touch, and focused attention—you will know you have a teenager with a full emotional tank, ready to be trained and ready to leap forward in spiritual, mental, and emotional growth. You will have won a great part of the battle of parenting a teenager.

# 6

# discipline with love

IMAGINE A SERIES OF SNAPSHOTS IN YOUR FAMILY ALBUM. THESE pictures show highlights in the life of your child. On the first page we see a pucker-faced newborn infant in her mother's arms. As we leaf through the scrapbook, we can't help but notice the spectacle of human development: the tiny, helpless bundle slowly transforming into an intelligent adult, capable of making every decision for herself.

So many changes are highlighted in those pictures. Hair color may change from fair to dark. Her first wobbly steps somehow become a graceful wedding procession. You helped her ride a bicycle, and now she helps you use the computer. That line of photographs captures one precious human being's all-important shift from being under your control to practicing self-control.

At the beginning she is completely dependent. If things go

well, then someday she will be fully independent, and she will have your full confidence. Guiding her from the starting line (control) to the finish line (self-control) is your ultimate goal as a parent.

A young child will see someone else's toy, try to grab it, and cry for it. She is governed only by her wants—and by your restraining hand. One day she will face more complex moral decisions, and your hope is that her personal self-control, rather than the iron grip of authority, will guide her choices.

It doesn't always happen that way, of course. It never has. But today, you and I observe a world where self-control seems almost quaint. Personal discipline seems to be taking a holiday. Married adults violate their vows by engaging in adulterous affairs at the office. People sell themselves into the slavery of severe financial debt because they want the big house now. People are urged to live by their feelings and appetites, and to "look out for number one." We now see around us a social consensus that sex without marriage is the norm, that frequent intoxication reflects the good life, and that self-restraint itself is outmoded and "puritanical." Meanwhile, nearly one in three Americans are overweight—a shocking statistical rise over the last two decades.[1] Why? Because we aren't learning self-control or personal discipline.

> We aren't learning self-control or personal discipline.

What are the patterns of discipline in your home? On a scale of 1 to 10, where a grade of 1 represents "highly permissive" and a grade of 10 represents "strict punishment," how would you evaluate your parenting style?

I believe we've experienced a tragic confusion about the subject of discipline. There have been two strands of extreme and opposite approaches to the subject, both of them damaging. On the one hand, we have seen the overly permissive strategy in which parents are reluctant to be firm. This strategy is largely motivated by a fear that firm boundaries could cause frustration in our children and drive them to rebellion. In some ways this is a natural reaction to the old-fashioned "woodshed" brand of authoritarian discipline. But as a result, we see a generation of children with no boundaries running wild, lacking the restraint that was never taught by parents. Permissiveness is not the same as love.

The other trend has come more recently, in the past two or three decades. We have seen a generation of parents reacting in the other direction, using a strict, authoritarian style. In other words, if children are running wild without discipline, then let's have more discipline. That was correct enough, but the problem came when *discipline was identified with punishment.* As we'll see later, these are two very separate concepts. Permission was replaced by punishment—an equal and opposite reaction. The authoritarian approach has conditioned children as if they were laboratory mice, quickly doling out negative reinforcement for any unwanted behavior and offering rewards and inducements for positive behavior. But what's wrong with that?

The problem is that just as punishment isn't the same as discipline, punishment isn't the same as love, either. It *does* train the child, and it trains with this message: "I love you and relate to you completely according to your behavior." The result has been an anger that has burrowed deep into the children, who then nurtured it until that anger reemerged in destructive and self-destructive ways. You might want to take a moment to review our discussion of passive-aggressive anger, the most dangerous anger of all. I believe stealth anger is the furnace of our currently angry world. And I think much of that anger can be traced to parents who meant well but who failed to understand the true nature of discipline. They punished away the bad behavior, but in doing so they created anger that filled the void where unconditional love should have been.

Because these are difficult but highly important problems, I trust you'll read and reflect on this chapter carefully.

## Yearning for Boundaries

By nature, children have a little streak of Calvin in them—meaning the young hero of the past comic strip *Calvin and Hobbes,* created by Bill Watterson. After a disappointing attempt to play organized baseball with other boys, Calvin creates a game called Calvinball to play with Hobbes, his imaginary tiger friend. The primary rule is that the game can never be played the same way twice. The rules of Calvinball "are subject to be changed, amended, or deleted by any player(s) involved. These rules are not required, nor necessary to play Calvinball." Furthermore, any player may declare a new rule at any point in the game, either vocally or silently.[2]

Naturally, Calvin often discovers the disaster inflicted by a boundless game. The absence of rules or defined playing areas can only lead to chaos. Teenagers realize this, no matter how much lip service they may give to their desire for freedom. All of us—adults included—test boundaries. You may have a strong distaste for traffic lights, but would you really enjoy driving through a big city without them?

Just bet on one proposition: your teenager will test the boundaries of permissiveness. That's simply what teenagers do; it's part of their biological job description. They are emerging from childhood into a new world of greater freedom and fewer limits; of more time and less supervision. Teenagers aren't certain where the end lines are, and the only way to find out is to push a toe curiously toward the end line. They have to test limits.

> **Teenagers aren't certain where the end lines are, and the only way to find out is to push a toe curiously toward the end line.**

Patricia Hersch has written a compelling book called *A Tribe Apart*. To write this book, she had to live apart herself, following and studying a group of teenagers over a long period. Her contention is that because of the nature of today's world—particularly with two working parents often the norm—today's teenagers are able to circumvent almost all adult supervision and live lonely lives in groups. Therefore, the need for moral guidance, supervision, and support—which she believes young people desire—goes unmet. Teens are a tribe apart, not because they have declared their independence, but because adults have abandoned them. They find little joy in all the extra freedom. They would trade it in an instant for our time, love, attention—and boundaries. Hersch pleads with parents to start paying better attention to their children.[3]

But parents are often uncomfortable with teenagers today. They protest that this is a generation of teenagers who are difficult to really know. Why is this? Hersch answers:

It's because we aren't there. Not just parents, but any adults. American society has left its children behind as the cost of progress in the workplace. This isn't about working parents, right or wrong, but an issue for society to set its priorities and to pay attention to its young in the same way it pays attention to its income . . . Adolescents are growing up with no adults around and no discussion about whether it matters at all.[4]

A recent government study of America's teenagers made an intriguing discovery. The basic finding, of course, was that parental involvement clearly keeps teens away from smoking, drinking, drug use, sexual activity, violence, and suicide attempts; and parental involvement clearly improves educational performance. The more striking conclusion related to one facet of family life: the dinner table. In each of these categories, there was a powerful correlation between families who ate dinner together and families who raised healthy and well-behaved teenagers. Also, the children of "dinner table families" consistently reported feeling close to their parents, while those who ate separately were far less likely to enjoy that closeness.[5]

For example, will your teenager use drugs? According to the study, 24 percent of "dinner table" teens will do so; for the "dinner apart" teens, the figure leaps to 50 percent. Teens ages fifteen to sixteen who don't eat dinner with their parents regularly are twice as likely to attempt suicide; those teens are twice as likely also to abuse alcohol.[6]

It would be simplistic to make too much over the dinner table. Nothing magic happens around that table other than good communication, eye contact, and family bonding. In too many homes, as families go their separate ways to their separate activities—computers, television, and so on—they stop making eye contact. They stop communicating. And it becomes far more difficult for a parent to guide a teenager.

## The Faithfulness Principle

The most primary need you must meet as a parent is simply to be there. It has been said that 80 percent of the formula for success is just showing up. You won't always have your precious child in your home. Seize the day while you can. Find opportunities to be intricately involved in the life of your child. You can't train and teach boundaries if you aren't there. What you must establish is a pattern that matches the progression of those photographs. As your teenager grows and matures, you should gradually offer greater freedom and responsibilities. Move in a continuum from your control to her self-control.

Use the principle from Jesus's parable. The master gave his servant an assignment, then returned to evaluate the result. When he found the results impressive he said, "'Well done, good and faithful servant! You have been faithful with a few things; I will put you in charge of many things. Come and share your master's happiness!" (Matthew 25:21). This is a biblical model for growth and maturity. We use the faithfulness principle in other places, such as the work world, simply because it makes sense. Why not help your teenager progress in the same positive and loving pattern?

There are many advantages to this approach. For one, it is positive and motivational. You offer the prize of your trust and of greater freedom and privilege. But it may be harder than you think. It's necessary to begin with rather tight restrictions so that you're left with plenty of room to reward obedience. Many parents make the mistake of being too permissive in the beginning. The teenager is bound to fail somewhere, and the parent must then take the negative step of increasing restrictions. Training your teen is always more fruitful when things are positive—when you're able to say, "Well done, good and faithful teenager!"

Therefore it's very important—and not always easy—to begin with tighter restrictions, which mean easier goals for your child. She will also have a deeper appreciation for the rights and privileges she has earned. You've made a simple reward—permission to go on a camping trip with an approved friend, for example—a lesson in responsibility and trustworthiness. (In the next section I'll offer an example of how we used this principle with our daughter.)

> **A key lesson every teenager must learn is that actions have consequences.**

I'll say this again: it's harder than you think. You love your child, and you'll frequently be tempted to offer unearned rewards. Pressure from other teenagers and other parents will also enter into the equation. Remember that your great goal is a young person who is responsible, trustworthy, and independent by the age of eighteen—and that the "nice" way isn't always the loving way.

Remember also what Patricia Hersch discovered in her deep discussions with many teenagers. They want the boundaries. They see love in limits, though they will never tell you so. They've certainly told me as I've counseled with them. I've heard many times from young people that they felt their parents must not love them because they were not strict or firm enough.

## Actions and Consequences

A key lesson every teenager must learn is that actions have consequences. As simple as that sounds, every individual must learn through experience. There are many adults today who don't understand the consequences of their actions, whether those actions be adultery, running up credit card debt, or even simple overeating. As you set the boundaries and the goals for your teenager's growth toward increased responsibility, you'll need to be clear in establishing consequences that are consistent and fair. It's too easy—and too harmful—to figure out punishments when we're emotionally upset over our children's behavior. Our teenagers observe us as being impulsive and inconsistent. You need to be logical and well-planned in your responses. How?

Begin with the word *why*. Your teenager wants to know why she can't go to that party, for example. I believe every teenager is entitled to know the reason for our guidelines—but not entitled to a lengthy argument to swing the decision. So when your teenager asks why, give a practical reason. Teenagers understand and appreciate practical reasons more than moralistic ones. We do need to touch on the moral point of view, but we also need to remember that teenagers are in the thick of working out their own values. They're questioning our moral guidelines. So it's a good idea to be clear about practical reasons.

At the age of twelve, our daughter Carey decided she was ready for dating. Every parent knows what it feels like to hear that announcement! What . . . already?

We told Carey that it wasn't going to happen as of yet.

Her question: *When?*

Our answer: *When you're ready—about four years from now, give or take.*

Her question: *How will you know I'm ready?*

Our answer: *When you've learned to function comfortably in groups.*

Her question: *Why?*

And I carefully explained that many teenagers fail to learn how to be part of a group. That failure follows them into adulthood, and they become socially miserable. "No daughter of mine is going to be a social misfit!" I declared. We told Carey that when she accomplished that goal, we would talk about larger social privileges.

Social ease is a practical point any teenager can understand. And notice that Pat and I left room for error and judgment, rather than saying something like, "On your sixteenth birthday." We gave a practical goal and a broad time frame, with strong motivation for our child to grow socially and emotionally.

One year later Carey came to us again with the subject. She wanted us to know she had learned to operate in groups. And indeed she had. At this point we acknowledged and affirmed her success. But we told her that there was more to functioning in a group than simply getting along with everyone. We needed to make positive contributions and provide leadership at this point. "Carey," we said, "you're doing great. But we'd like to see you become a leader—someone who has a positive influence on others in your circle." This was not a *new* goal for Carey but a more advanced portion of the goal we had already given her.

She understood this, and she set to work. How proud we are of the emotional maturity our daughter gained as she became a warm, wholesome, gentle, and positive group member who was ready for the new challenge of dating. And at that point we knew we could trust her to make the right decisions.

## The Partnering Parent

Let's return for a minute to that continuum—the transition of your child moving from your control to her own self-control. I've discovered that the parent's attitude, particularly as it comes across to the teenager, is extremely important in how the teen will respond. She has a powerful motivation to gain freedom and privileges during this period. How will she see your part in the process?

I've seen many parents act in an attitude of fear and prevention that comes across in a very negative way to their teenagers. The parent comes to be seen as an obstacle blocking the way to freedom and adulthood. The parent may desperately strive to keep his or her child dependent on parents and authority. This predisposes the child to becoming passive and dependent as an adult—someone easily manipulated by others.

On the other hand, we've already discussed the problem of being overly permissive. The parent throws open the door, establishes no boundaries, and the child actually feels unloved.

So what should your approach be? You want your child to see you in this regard as a kind of partner in a common goal. She wants to become an independent and mature young adult, and you want that for her too. Why not work together, hand in hand? Why not clearly explain that your goal is for her to move from complete dependence upon you to wise, deserving independence? Again, that's a practical point any teenager can understand. And you become not an obstacle but an essential guide and enabler toward a positive future. You're still the one in control, and your teen needs and wants you to be in control for now. But it's a very loving and gentle kind of control, clearly guided toward what is best for the teenager. She needs to be reminded from time to time that you are working together toward her gradual freedom, which will be given as she proves ready.

Once I was counseling the parents of a sixteen-year-old boy named Randy. The latest crisis was his desire to go to a concert that had all kinds of unwholesome baggage attached to it. His

parents had been carefully expressing to him their desire to gradually give him more and more independence. They had explained
that there would be some requests for which they could not give
permission because he wouldn't be ready. Randy's parents had
done everything right, but
he was still pleading with
them about going to the
concert. It had become a
tremendous issue between
them. Worrying about his
anger and frustration, the
parents almost gave in.

> **Teenagers need parents to be in control at all times, or they will lose the sense of security.**

This would have been a mistake not only because the concert
was unhealthy, but because "caving in" damages the parent-child
relationship. Teenagers want boundaries. They need parents to be
in control at all times, or they will lose the sense of security.

Randy was sixteen and a half. This is a year particularly loaded
with these kinds of judgment calls. Teenagers are receiving their
driver's licenses. They are awake to all the possibilities of the
world, and they have a premature sense of independence. Parents,
of course, have new reason to worry when their child's hands
eagerly wrap around a steering wheel. Randy's parents realized
they had only eighteen months available for training before their
son became a "legal adult." They wanted him to be emotionally
and intellectually ready to make good decisions.

Randy's parents did the right thing—they explained that very
directive to him. Most of the time a teenager will respond well to
such a careful, respectful offering of the facts. When he does continue to oppose you, simply explain that until his eighteenth
birthday, you reserve the right to have the final say. I hope you

don't reach that kind of standoff, and that you won't need to assert your authority. But sometimes it's necessary. Simply do so in a way that demonstrates your loving motives, and you should be able to forestall anger.

There are also some positive steps you can take. By all means, use positive training whenever you can. For example, provide a small checking account for your teenager, complete with modest monthly deposits. Share the parable of the faithful servant in Matthew 25 and add, "I want you to take on the challenge of learning to handle money." Start with a few very minor expenses, and let her earn the right to be "faithful in larger things."

It's also very positive to discuss the future together. Sit down with her occasionally and ask her about her hopes and dreams. Where does she want to go to college? What kind of vocation does she envision for herself? This allows you to help her investigate the facts about schools and careers. As you do so, you're doing much more than simply distributing information. You're demonstrating through focused attention that you really care about her future and her desires. Then, if and when you do need to make the difficult decision, she will understand your love and support—and she is far more likely to submit to your wisdom.

## Setting Limits

Every parent wants to know the answer to this question: "How much restriction should I impose on my teenager when she has misbehaved?"

I want to emphasize fairness, common sense, and letting the punishment fit the crime. I can recall a situation in which parents grounded their son at home for one year because he had gone to a bar. You can imagine the anger such an overreaction could create—and the desire to rebel by going to bars again as soon as he was practically able to do so. Surely a "lesser crime" should carry a lower penalty. If your daughter comes in fifteen minutes past curfew after her date, then a few days of restriction should be sufficient. If it happens again, of course, the penalty should be lengthened. It's my observation that a penalty period of more than two weeks is rarely necessary; four weeks would represent an extreme outside limit. If you come to the point where you're having to dole out regular penalties, and you have a "repeat offender" in your home, then that's a flashing red light to tell you something is wrong in your home, in your relationship with your child, in the teenager's private life, or some other area. We'll discuss this later in the book.

Every parent has to make the determination of what boundaries and what restrictions apply to a given situation. Be loving, be proactive in establishing clear limits, and use common sense. Remember that if you keep your teenager's emotional tank full, your chances of dealing with misbehavior will become much smaller. The well-loved teenager returns love partially by pleasing her parents. Love is your greatest ally.

## Power, Love, and Self-Discipline

Let me close this chapter by urging you to discipline with love. Discipline is positive guidance. It is not the same as punishment, which is a last resort. Your work with your teenager is a labor of love—not the "breaking of a wild stallion." We might train an animal by breaking its spirit, but we train a child by loving her toward her greatest potential for wisdom, productiveness, emotional maturity, integrity, and happiness. You are not working against your child but with her, toward a common goal that will bring great pleasure and fulfillment to you both.

In the Bible Paul points out that the best athletes exhibit incredible self-discipline as they train—and for a much more temporal reward: an earthly trophy. Our trophy, he says, is "a crown that will last forever" (1 Corinthians 9:25). The lessons and the wisdom that come through during this time will not fade. Help your teenager understand that the athlete is often tired, sore, and uncomfortable. He strains under the burden of the training room. But he is there because he wants to be the best he can be. He wants to win that crown. For

**Discipline is positive guidance.**

that reason, even when his muscles ache and his brow is drenched with sweat, he feels good inside. He knows there is no shortcut to a championship.

Disciplining a teenager has its own moments of discomfort and pain. There will be tears, disagreements, and disappointments. Love is the glue that will hold it all together in these times—and season everything with your parental self-control. God gives us "a spirit of power, of love and of self-discipline" (2 Timothy 1:7). If parent and teen can simply keep that perspective, keep their "eyes on the prize," and keep moving forward, the training period can be a positive time that will be fondly remembered.

Author and therapist Larry Crabb draws a sharp distinction between his ideas of discipline and self-control. He defines *personal* discipline as a matter of willpower—the ability to restrain oneself when it's the logical thing to do. It is a necessary negative. But, he says, "self-control is a decision that comes from deep

within. It's something you really want to do as opposed to deny-
ing what you want to do . . . That, to me, is a huge difference:
rigid discipline versus freedom—the freeing fruit of the Holy
Spirit."[7] Self-control, as he sees it, is a positive thing.

That's a good expression of a healthy goal for the young adults
we will one day present to the world. Their self-control should not
be painful and frustrating, but joyful. They will be faithful to their
marriages with no reluctance at all, but with the sheer wisdom of
knowing that faithfulness brings contentment while the alternative brings pain and brokenness. They will be law-abiding citizens
who make their communities better, not because they grit their
teeth and force themselves, but because it gives them tremendous
pleasure and satisfaction. They will serve God always in love,
never in fear. Isn't this what we want for our children, fellow parent? Isn't this what we want for ourselves?

Imagine the day when your children join you, their loving parents, at the pinnacle of maturity when Christ looks at your family and says, "I no longer call you servants, because a servant does
not know his master's business. Instead, I have called you friends"
(John 15:15). At the end of all the guidance and discipline, it's
time to celebrate.

At that point, we smile in the knowledge that all our efforts
were worthwhile after all.

# 7

# protecting your teenager

CHAP CLARK IS ASSOCIATE PROFESSOR OF YOUTH, FAMILY, AND Culture at Fuller Theological Seminary. He has studied today's teenagers with care and a fresh insight. Much like Patricia Hersch, he has gathered his data from close range, interviewing many young people who consistently expressed hurt and longing amid the cultural rubble of today.[1] His conclusions are both alarming and hopeful.

Clark echoes Patricia Hersch as he identifies the real problem of teenagers today: "Adolescents have been cut off for far too long from the adults who have the power and experience to escort them into the greater society. Adolescents have been abandoned."[2] That is, modern parents are too involved with themselves and their careers. They are too busy, and without realizing it, they've thrown their children to the wolves of an angry world.

Yet as frightening as this scenario may seem, Clark gives us a helpful thought: "The biggest need every student has is satisfied in one adult who is there for him or her."[3]

I believe those words, don't you? I believe that one truly loving parent—and certainly a pair of them—can stand in the gap against the greatest dangers that threaten a young person. There is no television show, Internet site, video game, or classroom incident that can compare to the influence you have over your own teenager. He looks to you all the more as he looks out in confusion on a world even more confused than he is. Your message of love, morality, integrity, and biblical wisdom will shine against the darkness he sees around him.

> **Modern parents are too busy, and without realizing it, they've thrown their children to the wolves of an angry world.**

Therefore, as we discuss the practical issues of protecting our teenagers, let's do so with confidence that this battle can be won. As servants of the truth, we need not fear. "For God has not given us a spirit of fear, but of power and of love and of a sound mind" (2 Timothy 1:7 NKJV).

We must protect our children in the social realm (friends, activities) as well as in the sensory realm (media, education, culture). In this chapter we'll primarily discuss the social realm, which every teenager views as the great frontier.

## The Parent Network

A teenager looks out on the world with fascination. Up to now, the family unit has encompassed his whole life. Mother and

Father loomed like giants, filling all his needs. Yes, he had friends in the neighborhood or on the playground. He may have taken part in Little League sports or scouting, but the home was always his true world. You spent that time building for him a loving foundation that would provide him the strength and training he would need to someday leave and be an effective adult himself.

That time to leave has not yet come—relax! However, adolescence is the time for testing the waters of the outside world. Like a nervous child edging closer to the swimming pool, he is going to dip in a toe; then a foot; then a leg. He is going to experience that chilly sensation of moving into a new realm, where all the rules are different. This is the primary objective of the adolescent years: learning one's place as a social creature. Don't be alarmed when he suddenly wants to spend every possible moment with friends. Parents can be taken aback when their child first asks if he can stay home and wait for a friend's phone call rather than go out for a hamburger or pizza with his family. It's a healthy sign—a standard rite of passage.

From your perspective as a parent, things are about to grow more complicated. You're no longer in control of his every moment. Naturally, you're concerned whether he will "do everything right" on these little experimental excursions into the social world. And what if you're not too certain about those other families who are involved?

Your first move should be to establish good relationships with those other parents. You will find that time after time a tight network of parents can help one another make the best decisions. Your teenager will come to you breathless with excitement about a big party. "*Everyone* is going," he'll exclaim. What if you don't know the family hosting this party? What if you don't know the details? The remedy is a simple one! I have a difficult time in understanding why so many parents won't take a moment to use the telephone and gather some information. Don't they want all available information about the situations their teenager will encounter?

First of all, find like-minded parents who are concerned about protecting their teenager from dangerous influences. You'll find them in school parenting organizations, and you'll find them at your church. Introduce yourself and establish a relationship. These folks will be invaluable to you as you work together in sharing information and supporting one another in the decisions you make for your teenagers.

You also need to know the parents and friends who come into contact with your teenager. I can recall a time when our Carey, then fifteen, wanted to attend a party. We called her friend's mother, who was the hostess. Her response to my questioning was noticeably hostile. She said, "It's a private party, Dr. Campbell. Your daughter is welcome to come or to stay home. Her choice. But what we do in our own home is our business."

I knew simply from the mother's attitude that regardless of what they "did" in that home, it was no place for my teenager. Still, it was important to get the facts, so I pressed for details. It's always important to be polite and friendly. I said, "I understand. But I'm sure you can understand how we're careful about our daughter's activities, and we like to know a few details before she goes somewhere. Can you tell me a little about the party?"

I discovered that teenagers would be served wine and Bloody Marys at this party, in a sensually provocative atmosphere. You might be surprised to discover what often happens at teenage parties today, particularly when you know that these activities are sanctioned by parents. Coed sleepovers are very common, for example. Boys and girls bring sleeping bags or "crash" on a sofa, and they all sleep in the same room—supposedly under the watchful eye of parents,

> **Your goal is to help your teenager make sound moral decisions.**

who surely fall asleep at some point. *Teen People* magazine polled 879 young people and found that just over half had attended a coed sleepover. Even more alarming, 83 percent said they had either seen or heard about their friends engaging in sexual activity at such an event.[4]

Remember that your goal is to help your teenager make sound moral decisions. But at a time when hormones are raging and parents' values are being questioned, it's a terrible mistake to let your child be exposed to such a level of temptation. Carey was trustworthy at the time of the party I described. She intended to behave maturely, and I'm certain she would have done so. But why place her in such an arena? Notice also that we're talking about situations *supervised by parents*. That's not enough today. Just because "moms and dads will be around," you can't necessarily rest easy. Get all the information you can—that's what protection is all about.

It's interesting to discover the kind of protection our own heavenly Father provides for us:

> So, if you think you are standing firm, be careful that you don't fall! No temptation has seized you except what is common to man. And God is faithful; he will not let you be tempted beyond what you can bear. But when you are tempted, he will also provide a way out so that you can stand up under it. (1 Corinthians 10:12–13)

To paraphrase these words, "In a tempting situation, don't have any illusions about your willpower! Everyone has the same temptations, but God is good. He won't put you in a situation that is too big for you to handle. And when you do find yourself challenged, look for the escape hatch that God always provides." It's a model of good supervision, isn't it? Don't place your children in situations too tough for them. Don't have illusions about their strength, no matter how proud of them you may be. And train them to walk away when the heat is on.

> **In a tempting situation, don't have any illusions about your willpower!**

## The Art of Delay

I fully understand how difficult some of your decisions will be. Even the best of parents struggle to know what to do in some situations—and the answer isn't always black or white. You're giving your teenager privileges based on a firm understanding of trust. He knows what is expected, he knows his boundaries, and he understands they are not arbitrary but carefully considered. Still, you are going to face decisions that are hard to make. I want you to understand that there is no reason you should make a "snap judgment." Wisdom isn't measured by speed. This is why delaying your decision can come in handy. Take a little extra time, and you'll be amazed how new and important facts come to light.

Our Carey was invited on a swimming trip. She was to spend the day with her friends on a large boat, then enjoy an "onboard party" that evening. This occurred that same year Carey was fifteen, at mid-adolescence when so many of these "tough calls" seem to emerge. My wife, Pat, and I simply weren't certain about this one. We weren't bothered by the daytime activities, but something about that evening party just didn't sit right with us. Yet there wasn't quite enough reason for us to refuse. We did, after all, know that the supervising parents were good and sensible people.

This was just the right time to delay: a situation where your intuition gives you doubts, but you can't quite be certain. The best thing to do is tell your teenager, "I'm not so sure, honey. Give me some time to think it over." Sometimes, given the transience of teenagers, the question answers itself rather quickly. Circumstances change or the teenager forgets all about her latest obsession and moves on to something else. Sometimes the delay will even cause the teenager to have second thoughts and withdraw her request for permission.

So I delayed my decision with Carey. Of course, she said, "Okay, but hurry! I have to know by Thursday."

By Thursday nothing had changed. Pat and I were uncertain, the weather looked great for the outing, and Carey was still intent on going. Now Carey pressed us for an answer. "Greg has to know tonight, Daddy. Can I go or not?"

As I've said, when we reveal a decision to a teenager, we owe it to them to give a practical reason (though we don't owe them a long argument). At the same time, I knew that Carey's behavior had been very good. I wanted to be fair, despite my negative intuition about the swimming party. So I was just on the verge of saying yes when Carey said, "By the way . . ."

I believe I've pointed out already that those are very significant words in the ear of a parent.

"By the way," Carey said, "Greg can't get his folks's car for this party. We have to go in his dune buggy—you know, the one with no seat belts. And, of course, we'll be crossing the bridge during five o'clock traffic."

I then had the right reason to deny permission for that party. How did Carey respond? She walked directly to the phone, called Greg, and said, "I'm sorry, my parents won't let me go."

Would you have expected my daughter to give me an argument? Would you have expected her to ask why she wasn't permitted to go to the swimming party?

I believe this was an instance of a teenager putting out a clue at just the right moment—giving her parents leeway to say no. It was Carey herself who raised the issue of the dune buggy and the traffic concerns. I think she was looking for a way out, but it can be difficult for a teenager to say no. Believe it or not, there are times when they welcome their parents' saying it for them.

Let's state it again: teenagers want boundaries. They want us to identify the boundaries and be consistent with them. Our decision let Carey off the hook with her friends, and it produced a sense of camaraderie between her and us. As long as your reasons are good, and you're not being untruthful in any way, you can draw closer to your teenager when they come to you looking for an escape route.

It may even be that my "intuition" about the party was really an ability to sense Carey's discomfort in being faced with that social setting. It's impossible to tell. But I believe that "delay tactics" helped protect our daughter from an unwholesome situation in that case. It has been said that fools rush in where angels fear to tread. With that in mind, parents should not be in any hurry to make decisions that are important elements in the maturity process of their teenager.

## The Transfer of Power

In the final analysis, the task of protection is passing on the responsibility to the one you are protecting. So many disagreements over rights and privileges become moot points as the teenager comes to see the world as his parent sees it. What is your greatest risk? Perhaps it is the risk of overprotection. You will have an undefeated record of victory in the smaller threats, but you will eventually lose the greater war. After all, you can't lock your teenager up forever. You can't accompany him on every date, select his spouse, and raise his children for him. At some point the essential transfer of wisdom must occur. Rules and regulations can go only so far before the state of the teenager's maturity sets his final destiny.

This can be a crisis for Christian parents. They are driven by virtue and value, and they have the best of intentions in shielding their child from the evil and corruption of this world. But they can become so vigilant that they are overprotective. Their teenager could become a passive young adult, incapable of making his own decisions. Or he could grow rebellious and begin looking for every opportunity to push out the walls of what feels like imprisonment.

It's not an easy thing, is it? On the one hand we have overprotection, which can stifle the spirit and fail to train the child in wisdom and discernment. On the other hand there is underprotection, the folly of so many "worldly" parents today, to use the

> **Rules and regulations can go only so far before the state of the teenager's maturity sets his final destiny.**

biblical vernacular. Underprotection can become an exercise in handing over the sheep to the wolves.

Nobody said your task would be easy! Keep in mind, however, that many parents are succeeding beautifully today. Remember the basics: Love your child, train him in anger management, and remember the great continuum that ranges from *your* control to the young adult's control. That means beginning with full, watchful protection over a child and ending with a child ready and willing to handle himself with wisdom and integrity in a challenging world. I trust and pray that as you devote your parenting to the eternal Parent, and take it one day at a time, your teenager's eighteenth birthday will be as much a day of joy for you as for your child. For by this time, you will be able to present the world with a spiritually and emotionally healthy young adult who is trustworthy in making decisions. You won't lose a wink of sleep over his character, and you'll glow with pride as he establishes his own unique path in the world.

That's certainly our long-range goal, isn't it? But for now, there are many challenges and troubling issues. Today's parents particularly ask me about issues of the media and pop culture. Therefore I've added the following chapter to help you think about these special challenges and to equip you with some resources to make the right decisions for your family.

# 8

# mind vs. media

IMAGINE, IN YOUR LIVING ROOM, THE GRAPHIC, EXTENDED SCENE of a teenage orgy.

The air date was December 31, 2004. The medium was television, brought to you by the CBS network and the series *Without a Trace*.

Just a few years ago, who would have thought that broadcast standards would dip so low? We depended on the vigilant protection of the Federal Communications Commission (FCC) and its media watchdogs. There were sights and words and ideas that we didn't have to worry about our children encountering. There were still a few shows that espoused decency and traditional, wholesome values. It's quite a plummet from, say, *Father Knows Best* (1950s) and *The Cosby Show* (1980s) to what has arrived in modern fare such as *Without a Trace*.

But far more outrageous were the backroom shenanigans. It came to light that the FCC had made a quiet deal with Viacom, the production company for *Without a Trace*. Viacom simply paid $3.5 million, and the FCC disregarded seventy thousand indecency complaints filed by taxpayers. "The FCC has sold out the American public," said Tim Wildmon, chairman of the American Family Association.[1]

Then, having paid their way out of accountability, CBS and Viacom demonstrated arrogance beyond imagining. They showed the teenage orgy episode *again*, on its third anniversary of airing, December 31, 2004.[2] Why not? It was a win/win situation for the network and the government agency. CBS made more money on publicity and advertising than a fine would cover; the FCC could receive extra funding through slap-on-the-wrist penalties.

> We must teach and train amid a cultural backdrop more pervasively immoral and hedonistic than ever before.

But shows such as *Without a Trace* aren't wins for your family—not as you struggle to raise your teenager in a healthy, moral atmosphere. Today we face challenges brand-new to parenting. We must teach and train amid a cultural backdrop more pervasively immoral and hedonistic than ever before. The alert parent must keep an eye on the TV screen.

Did you know that according to researchers from the Ohio State University School of Public Health in Columbus, one in nine high-school students sells drugs?[3] The alert parent must keep an eye on the high school hallway.

Did you know that two hundred thousand Americans are

addicted to pornography on the Internet?[4] Or that nine out of ten children between eight and sixteen years of age have viewed pornography on the Internet—often unintentionally?[5] The alert parent must keep an eye on technology.

Did you know that the latest teenage social fad is the NCMO: the "non-committal make-out session"? These parties are increasingly popular *with church kids* who don't want to "go all the way" but still prefer their love lives to be quick, convenient, and impersonal.[6] The alert parent must keep an eye even on church parties.

There can be little doubt that profit-driven advertisers have taken on a powerful voice of authority in our culture—and young people listen. It is the carefully contrived voice of what a PBS special called "The Merchants of Cool," calculated to win the ears (and weekly allowances) of impressionable teenagers.

Are we overreacting? Not according to one prominent culture-watcher:

> Often there's a kind of official and systematic "rebelliousness" that's reflected in media products pitched at kids. It's part of the official rock video world view, it's part of the official advertising world view, that your parents are creeps, teachers are nerds and idiots, authority figures are laughable, [and] nobody can really understand kids except the corporate sponsor. That huge authority has, interestingly enough, emerged as the sort of tacit superhero of consumer culture. That's the coolest entity of all.[7]

These facts are not cited to cause alarm. My greatest desire is to encourage and energize you as a parent with this book. But as molders of young minds, we can't afford to hide from the cold truth that today's culture is filled with moral peril. On many levels—socially, mentally, emotionally, spiritually, educationally, and physically, to name a few—we have to be vigilant in protecting our teenagers at an age when their hearts and minds are still being formed, and are therefore fragile.

## Teens and the Internet

As we've already seen, Internet pornography is freely circulating in our world. As many as twenty million adults visit cybersex sites each month, and studies show that one-third of all men with Internet access—and almost that percentage of *ministers*—visit pornographic sites.[8] One consequence of adult enslavement to any source is that the adult will be ineffective in training a child to avoid the same enslavement.

Teenagers are curious about sexuality. You must remember from your own experience that sexuality is a dominant, almost obsessive interest during adolescence. Hormones are coming to life and sending all kinds of signals. But no past generation of teenagers has had to cope with the quiet, seductive lure of the Internet. It promises anonymity! The teen can investigate in the privacy of his own home—perhaps even his bedroom, unless you're proactive in performing good preventive maintenance.

"Cyberporn Alley," of course, is the worst and most unhealthy place your teenager could possibly visit. The effects of pornography on healthy spiritual, social, and emotional development have been well documented. An ounce of prevention is worth untold pounds of cure in this case. And your very first move should be to arm yourself with all the information you possibly can. That information includes just a small bit of technological savvy. If you are convinced you're incapable of handling computers and simple program adjustments, then it's imperative that you find someone in your church or your neighborhood who can help you.

First, I would recommend keeping the computer in a place where you have easy access to it. Many teenagers today have their own computes, and they like to keep them in their bedrooms where they can play games, surf the Internet, and so forth. This is one more area of trust your teenager will need to earn, and it should in no way be easily attained—the stakes are too high, given the dangers of the Net. Even then, if your teen keeps a computer in his room, it should be connected to a home network where you can easily supervise his activities. Or you should visit the room frequently to check. Your teen may complain about your intrusion of his privacy. Be loving and gentle about these checks, explaining that some dangers outweigh privacy.

Second, several software tools make it possible for you to be the master of the computers in your home. These include activity monitors; cache explorers; site-filtering software; spyware-removal software; and personal firewalls. But always remember that teens often keep one step ahead of adults when it comes to the latest software and technology. If you install an activity monitor, for example, a clever teen may go to a site such as www.download.com and try to download a program that hides his browsing activity. Naturally, there are young hackers who create all kinds of programs to further unscrupulous and immoral use of the Internet.[9]

At any rate, be sure to learn about:

## Activity Monitors

You can purchase or download simple programs that make it possible for you to log all Internet activity. You can quickly see

what Web sites have been visited, as well as the content of
e-mails, chats, and other activities. Examples can be found at
http://www.spectorsoft.com, but shop around and search for
your own best solutions.

## Cache Explorers

Your Web browser (such as Internet Explorer, Netscape
Navigator, or Mozilla Firefox) keeps a "cache" of activities, similar
to the activity monitor mentioned above. Browsers also keep cache
information under "history" in the options menu. The teenager
can easily erase his tracks from the cache, so remember you'll need
more than one way of checking up.

## Site-Filtering Software

Site-filtering software lets you predetermine what kind of
sites can be visited by your computer. The software preanalyzes a
Web site and, if it finds certain terms, blocks it out. Obviously
this is another imperfect system in that it will occasionally block
a legitimate site when finding those words present—for example,
one that gives you information about this very subject. Cyber
Patrol, by Surf Control Inc. and Cybersitter, by Solid Oak
Software Inc. are two highly rated programs for filtering sites.
Also, you should be familiar with your browser's built-in settings.
On Microsoft's Internet Explorer, select "Tools" from the menu
at the top; then select "Internet Options"; then "Content". You
will be instructed how to activate the "Content Advisor" and
restrict certain kinds of sites. For other browsers and for a wealth
of updated information on this subject, visit the Internet
Content Rating Association at http://www.icra.org/.

## Spyware Removal

Be certain your teenager understands that one of the dangers of Internet pornography is "Trojan horse" factor: damaging viruses and spyware programs sneak into your system via pornographic media (or sometimes other downloads). This fact can actually become a deterrent for your teenager because he would be humiliated to have his furtive activities exposed through a damaged computer-operating system. Spyware allows a third party to secretly track your computer's activities and possibly some of your personal information—credit card numbers, for example. Many teens have used the KaZaA program for sharing MP3 music files over the Internet while that program included spyware. Ad-Aware by Lavasoft is a fine program for removing spyware.

## Firewalls

There are firewalls available as both hardware and software. The latest Microsoft operating systems have built-in firewalls, but you need to be certain you understand the workings of your firewall. It can prevent your computer from being "hacked" or invaded over the Internet by an outside user. It will generally alert you, the user, when one of your programs is attempting to use the Internet or when someone on the outside is trying to connect with your computer. Any sensible user of the Internet should have a good working firewall. Norton Utilities provide firewalls, virus security, and other effective maintenance tools.

> Software can be very helpful, but it cannot replace the effectiveness of good communication between a parent and a child.

Software can be very helpful, but it cannot replace the effectiveness of good communication between a parent and a child. For one thing, you can't regulate your teenager's activities when he is at a friend's home or some other place. You need good communication and good training.

Share information together about computers and sexuality. Explain to your teenager that there are three serious dangers relating to Internet pornography: physical (predators who attempt to lure your teenager to a face-to-face meeting); emotional/spiritual (exposure to unhealthy and addictive influences); and practical (invasion of privacy through hacking). Just as automobiles are too dangerous to be made available to us when we are too young, the Internet is dangerous too. It can be a healthy, educational, and fun process, but it should be made available only through a parent's personal supervision.[10]

We should also remember that a teenager can limit his activities to relatively healthy sites and still be "addicted" to the Internet. Some teenagers spend hours every day visiting game sites or chatting through programs like AOL Instant Messenger or e-mail. The Internet is a curious phenomenon: it opens the world to us, yet simultaneously isolates us. Your teenager needs a healthy balance of physical activities, reading, schoolwork, and development of his special talents and abilities. We'll say more about this in our section on motivation.

## Teens and the Tube

We now come to the monster conglomerate known as the current media—television, movies, music, and video games. We cannot afford to be naive about the powerful influence these media have over our children, even in families with effective parents. More than ever, this is a consumer society with an uncurbed appetite for financial profit, even when it means infiltrating the mind and tastes of your child.

The powers who control our entertainment have the imperative of motivating us to spend, then spend some more. They will attempt to sell you, say, the most enticing video game, then x number of its sequels—each of which must be more enticing and outrageous than the one preceding it. Who decides what television shows are aired? Profiteers, not a coalition of ministers. And because the TV networks are in competition with one another, they are not likely to select the most modest, healthy, and spiritually enriching programs. The most shocking and extravagant will attract the publicity and the viewers.

We all know by now that television has an extraordinary influence on young minds. Those who would dispute its power should consider why so many billions of dollars are spent on TV advertising—someone believes that running those commercials will sell products. The question is, what are the less-tangible "products" being sold by the shows and the stars of Hollywood today? Sex, materialism, and power would head the list. Studies have found that television viewing is associated with aggression, a desensitization to violence, and increased fear.[11] Against an increasing outcry from parents and family organizations, television finally took some steps to police itself during the 1990s. The Telecommunications Act of 1996 declared that televisions be manufactured with a "V-chip," which allowed parents to block offensive TV programs based on a careful television rating system. All programs other than news and sports would receive ratings, then parents could set their V-chips based on the ratings.

There were three major problems with this system. First, the initial ratings were based not on content but on someone's perceived idea of what was "age appropriate." Many parents would disagree with the MPAA (Motion Picture Association of America) on what, for example, was healthy for a twelve-year-old viewer. Second, most parents opted to ignore the V-chip. This was a sad development, demonstrating that more of us are willing to complain about a problem than to make the effort to take charge of it. Surveys demonstrated that most parents had no idea there was a V-chip on their set—much less how to use it.

The third problem with the MPAA ratings and the V-chip was that without parental supervision, young people would be even more attracted to the wrong shows. The rating would simply call their attention to provocative programming.

By the way, it has also been observed that the MPAA ratings system only brought more sex, violence, and offensive language than ever. During the time the system was instituted, all of these negative factors increased.

> The family television must be cared for carefully, just as if it were a loaded weapon. The harm it does to younger minds and hearts is subtle, slow, and deadly.

I predict you're already aware of the most important solution to these problems. Parents need to take control of their own television sets. If there is a V-chip, know about it and know how to use it. If there are rating systems, pay attention and turn the channel when you need to. And don't simply send your children out of the room. Parents should set the example by avoiding the offending show themselves (teenagers are very sensitive to hypocrisy).

As with computers, be certain your television is in a common place, where private viewing won't take place. There was a time when we could simply ask parents to stay away from the so-called "premium channels" (HBO, Showtime, etc.) with their adult content. But today, it's truly amazing and disappointing to see the content that is available on standard channels at any hour of the day. Therefore the family television must be cared for carefully, just as if it were a loaded weapon. The harm it does to younger minds and hearts is subtle, slow, and deadly.

## Music, Movies, and Video Games

What about movies? DVD rentals are popular, so you can be aware of what your children are going to see, particularly in your own home. When your teenager goes to the movies, ask what the film will be. Check online to find out more about the movie. Let your teenager know it's a matter of integrity. Ask questions afterward to be certain your teenager really attended the film in question. Also, talk to other parents. Let them know that you're careful about the influences your teenager encounters. Later in this book we'll discuss a positive way to take charge of these issues of media influence: making your home a desirable destination for your teenager and his friends. That way you can enjoy a good, healthy DVD or television show together, while spending more time with young people.

Music is another questionable presence in the lives of our teenagers. It's harder than ever for adults to regulate, because teenagers share songs in the form of MP3 files. This can prevent you from being aware of the album ratings. The Recording Industry Association of America (RIAA) uses a "Parental Advisory: Explicit Lyrics" rating for certain albums.[12] Those, of course, should be avoided. As for other music, it can be fruitful and educational for you and your teenager to review lyrics together, as talking points. This is an excellent opportunity to train your teen to think biblically about cultural issues. Ask what the song is about. What is the songwriter's worldview? What is the listener being called upon to do? Does this song present a healthy view of the world and of life? Why or why not?

There is no shortage of healthy music your teenager may enjoy exploring—older music, classics, and Christian music. Teenagers today are eclectic in their interests, and they're very willing to "go retro," as they put it, and consider music from past eras. Surely this is partly because the current state of popular music seems spiritually and creatively bankrupt. It's true that teenagers often use music as one more way to signal their distinction from adults and adult culture. The fact that a song is loud or outrageous may be the whole point. Still, it's important to work on making music a "common ground" the family can enjoy together rather than a dividing wall to shut the adults out.

What about video games? Many teenagers are very interested in this form of entertainment. The major platforms for console games are Sony Play Station, Nintendo Gamecube, and Microsoft Xbox. Then, of course, there are PC games for the home computer and for the Apple McIntosh. There has been plenty of publicity about the outrageous violence allowed by this industry. The two teenagers who opened fire with machine guns in Columbine High School in Colorado were devotees of games such as *Doom* and *Quake*, where a "first-person shooter" moves through various environments and piles up random killings. Other games such as *Grand Theft Auto* involve cars running over pedestrians or some other expression of casual pretend violence. If your teenager expresses a desire to play such games, you should say no and give good, practical reasons for your decision. These games influence the mind in the same way as computer programming—more so, perhaps, because they are interactive instead of passive. What view of the value of human life is reflected in violent games? How enriching a use of time do these games offer?

While we're mentioning use of time, it's good to set limits on any use of media at home—particularly with television and the computer. One hour for either would be a good suggestion. In this way, a teenager will be required to make careful decisions about what show he wants to watch on television or how he wants to use computer time. Of course, computers can be used positively for homework requirements, and you might make an exception here.

## A Time to Rest

It has been documented that many teenagers are chronically fatigued in school. They lack sleep because, among other reasons, parents don't enforce reasonable bedtimes and because there are so many tempting media entertainment choices. A teenager wants to surf the Internet, cruise the cable television dial, or listen to an iPod through earphones. Research shows that teenagers get an average of 7.5 hours of sleep per day, while needing 9.25 to be optimally alert and ready to learn in school.[13] This is complicated by an adolescent shift in the human body's circadian clock. You may know it as the "biological clock," the inner timepiece that regulates sleepiness and wakefulness. During the teenage years it shifts

> **Research shows that teenagers get an average of 7.5 hours of sleep per day, while needing 9.25 to be optimally alert and ready to learn in school.**

toward later times, creating a biological desire to stay up later at night and to sleep later in the morning.[14]

As a matter of fact, teachers are complaining more frequently that students are drowsy or even asleep in morning classes. There has been a certain amount of success in moving back the starting time, with teenagers seeming more alert and ready to learn by 9:00 a.m. or so. But of course, we are mainly dealing with symptoms when we push back the day. Every parent needs to take a hard look at the family's use of time and resources. I would suggest an "electronic curfew" of the television, the stereo, and the computer after an appropriate hour. Once more, let your teenager earn more freedom in this direction. Set benchmarks for good grades, a good record of getting up on time, and other considerations. Today, it is as difficult for teenagers to go to sleep on time as it is to rise on time. That goes for parents too.

Remember that fatigue can be the enemy of all that you and your teenager need to accomplish together. Be certain that both of you are well rested and alert.

## Guiding the Mind

Only for so long can one hold back the flood by plugging a finger in the dike. It is a flood of cultural garbage that concerns us, and there are only so many ways we parents can keep it from seeping into our homes. What, then, is the ultimate solution? You need to help your teenager learn to see the world from a biblical perspective. We all need to see these sexually obsessed movies and Web pages, cynical television shows and the like, for what they are.

Begin with yourself. Do you and your spouse watch the kind of films you don't want your teenager to see? Think about the message: "Your parents enjoy this entertainment, but you cannot." As always, the parents are the models. They set the tone. Parents have a difficult time teaching against any kind of behavior—whether it's smoking, abuse of alcohol, or attention to a debased culture—while demonstrating its attractiveness for themselves. For some parents, the first order of business may be to clean up their own habits!

Having done so, address the state of the world's messages head-on. Look for opportunities to guide your teenager while pointing out the message in the medium. Imagine you're watching television together when a beer advertisement airs. Watch it together, and ask your teenager what messages are implied. It may be something such as, "Men who drink this brand of beer end up with the most attractive women." Once you bring that idea to the surface, everyone can see the silliness and irrationality of it. There are actually times when it's more effective to shine the light of reason on such a message rather than quickly change the channel and give the message a kind of forbidden allure. Other times, of course—an immoral television show, for example—it's best to change channels and find something better for the family to view.

> **For some parents, the first order of business may be to clean up their own habits!**

If you create the habit of examining the messages all around you, your child will do the same. It's worth remembering that teenagers hate hypocrisy and hidden manipulations of every kind. They are naturally attracted to sincerity and truth. So you'll be surprised how quickly they'll take the initiative in looking for the hidden and destructive messages.

Your family can adopt John's profound words as a theme:

> For everything in the world—the cravings of sinful man, the lust of his eyes and the boasting of what he has and does—comes not from the Father but from the world. The world and its desires pass away, but the man who does the will of God lives forever. (1 John 2:16–17)

Study that passage together. The short and direct letter of 1 John makes a wonderful study for families. Point out the three deadly tendrils of worldliness in this passage: bodily cravings, material cravings, and pride. Nearly all the advertisements (and movies, music, and TV shows are advertisements in their own way) are aimed at one of these. John tells us that these wither quickly. But those who serve God live forever. We are made for much greater pleasures.

As you help your teenager learn to see the world through a biblical lens, let me remind you to offer practical reasons along with moralistic ones. A growing teenage mind needs more than "because God said so." As you point out the irrationality and superficiality of the beer advertisement, for example, you can establish that this is one more of the "cravings of sinful man"— but at the same time, there are many good and practical reasons to abstain from the abuse of alcohol that our media glorify.

Tragically, there will be some in your community who die because of drunk driving. There will be lives ruined through alcoholism. Be certain to point out these obviously wise and sensible considerations when you discuss the errors of worldly messages.

In John Bunyan's novel, *The Pilgrim's Progress*, the characters Christian and Faithful make their way through the marketplace known as Vanity Fair. It is a picture of the world in any age, filled with lust, greed, and pride. First, the residents notice the shining garments of the two pilgrims. They also notice that the pilgrims seem to speak a different language entirely because they had been in the presence of God. And third, they notice that the pilgrims are not seduced by the wares of Vanity Fair. They are on too wonderful a journey to give in to passing and unworthy pleasures.

Fellow parent, I trust you're ready to walk with your teenager through the "vanity fair" of this world. The temptations are powerful and the danger is real, but the truth is on your side. So is the Lord, who desires your family to walk in the light together. By modeling the right values in your own life and helping your teenager discern the values he confronts in the world, you can raise a pure and wholesome young person, undefiled by the high toxicity of cultural pollutants.

> **A growing teenage mind needs more than "because God said so."**

Do not conform any longer to the pattern of this world, but be transformed by the renewing of your mind. Then you will be able to test and approve what God's will is—his good, pleasing and perfect will. (Romans 12:2)

# 9

## beyond the birds and the bees

MIDDLE SCHOOL GUIDANCE COUNSELOR PEGGY COOPER HAS an observation to share—and it's not very pleasant. She confides these revelations to the audience of the PBS special "The Lost Children of Rockdale County."

Cooper was chatting with her students about their weekend parties. The teenagers were shockingly frank in describing their favorite social event. One of the students had a home that was nearly always parent-free. Therefore the students congregated there and tuned the television to the Playboy Channel. Ten or twelve kids were present, according to the account.

Cooper asked, "Was everyone watching?"

Not only were they watching, one of the boys offered, they were "getting pretty good at it."

Cooper quickly asked, "Good at what?"

The boy shared that the "game" involved watching the Playboy Channel and imitating whatever actions were being demonstrated.

One student added, "Sometimes it's all mixed up and it's just, like, there might be three or four of us at one time, and it doesn't matter if you're two guys or two girls or a girl and a guy, it doesn't matter. You just have to do what they're doing."[1]

> **Parents seldom realize they are the greatest influences on their children when it comes to issues of sexuality.**

Now, the incident above is surely a worst-case scenario. Yet it happened, and furthermore it happened in the heart of the Bible Belt. Rockdale County is not a district of California but of Georgia.

Why begin the chapter with such an extreme example? I would not have you press the panic button because of a sensational television news report. Most parents are doing a far better job, and most teenagers are responding with stronger morality and maturity. All the same, it's important that we know just what is at stake; how far our culture has fallen; what kinds of destructive influences may be taking root just around the corner from the street where you live. We are one generation past the "free love" movement of the 1960s, and we can all observe the sour fruit of licentious times—times that are even more licentious. Did you notice the role of the parents in the anecdote above? We know two things about them:

1. They aren't there to supervise behavior.
2. The Playboy Channel is.

It's hard to imagine a more destructive scenario for raising teenagers. What is most confounding is that parents seldom realize they are the greatest influences on their children when it comes to issues of sexuality. In surveys, parents generally suggest that their children's friends have the most powerful influence. But teenagers themselves make it very clear that they look to their parents first. How unfortunate that parents undervalue their own power in molding the minds of their teenagers.[2]

Here is what our teenagers are telling us:

- Most teens (nearly nine in ten) say that it would be easier for them to postpone sexual activity if they were able to have more open, honest conversations about these topics with their parents.
- Yet nearly one in four of them say they have never discussed sex with their parents.
- Six out of ten teens say that their parents are their role models for healthy, responsible relationships.[3]

On the other hand, in the same survey, one in five *younger* adolescents (ages twelve to fourteen) reported attending boy-girl parties with no adults in the house. Worst of all, other research indicates that one in five of our teenagers have had sexual intercourse by the age of fourteen—and that in those cases, one-third of the parents were aware of it.[4]

## Reclaiming Godly Sexuality

As you can see, the stakes are high in the current world of teenage sexuality. And parents play a highly significant role in what does or does not develop. It's a difficult subject for most of us. Our reluctance to discuss sex is matched only by our culture's eagerness.

And therein lies the danger. At whose hands would you have your teenager educated about the godly gift of sexuality? The world has hijacked a beautiful attribute fashioned by God and documented in the first chapters of the book of Genesis. We know that our heavenly Father created us male and female, as complements and companions. He set forth marriage as the holy vessel for intimacy from the very beginning. The institution embodied in Adam and Eve was not only practical for work, friendship, and reproduction; it served as a very tangible picture of the union between human creatures and Creator. The universal church itself is presented in the Bible as the bride of Christ. Therefore, the biblical perspective is that both marriage and sexuality are sacred institutions designed for one other—far from the casual, recreation-driven sexuality the world recommends. So the most primary lesson your teenagers need to learn about sexuality is this: that it was an invention neither of Hollywood nor Madison Avenue. God created sexuality for his own purposes: for deep companionship, for filling the earth with children, and for intimate joy between husband and wife. The world creates nothing new—it either teaches or twists the truth God has already established.

We need to be training our children in these concepts early and often. As we discussed in our chapter on the media, we can make our point most powerfully by using the examples before us. As you are traveling in the car and see a billboard featuring a bikini-clad young woman, ask your teenager about the message. In what way is the advertiser using sexuality? The answer, of course, is for sheer sensory manipulation. The beauty of the human body is being devalued so that someone can sell a product (one that, more often than not, has nothing at all to do with bikinis or bodies).

There are other questions too. Ask your teenager why it is that the media use only images of "perfect" physical specimens. How does that make most young people feel? What values are disseminated, and what is the cost to fragile and impressionable young minds? For example, you may point out the rapid rise of eating disorders such as bulimia nervosa. It has been demonstrated that the causes of bulimia are often more psychological than physical. Young people in particular feel that self-worth comes only in being thin and having the right body measurements. Even with the rise of these disorders and their tragic consequences, there are more and more "reality shows" on television that are devoted to makeovers, plastic surgery, and the evaluation of human beings as if they were meat at the butcher counter.

> God created sexuality for his own purposes: for deep companionship, for filling the earth with children, and for intimate joy between husband and wife.

Ask your teenagers if they believe most people are better off for living in a culture saturated with that kind of media; if they believe television is better or worse with the illicit imagery it uses. You might be surprised by the answers you hear, for teenagers tend to be embarrassed by what they see in this regard. It is an awkward subject about which they are curious but still very uncomfortable. Early on, it's a good idea to help them realize why and how our cultural media are drowning them in this one subject.

Then, against that backdrop of a superficial and misdirected world, set the wonderful and inspiring conception of Jesus, who loves all people from the inside out rather than the outside in. The prophecy of Isaiah 53:2 offers this picture of the Savior: "He had no beauty or majesty to attract us to him, nothing in his appearance that we should desire him." When he took the form of humanity, he came as a servant instead of a superstar; a peasant instead of a power broker. The Gospels themselves give us no physical description, because it is irrelevant. Jesus taught that the heart and the soul determine who we really are. He often chose to spend his time with the least popular—the sick and the meek.

Can you see the tremendous appeal such a figure has for a teenager? Jesus stood above social conventions and superficial evaluations. He chose truth, and the truth was that God loves us unconditionally rather than based on what we earn through appearance, deeds, or any other form of slavery. He loves us with a love that cannot be lost. If you can teach the powerful positives of Christ, you won't have to depend upon the nagging negatives of why we should turn off the television or boycott the movies. In other words, teach the underlying values because they are appealing and attractive. In the end, the best thing we have going for us is that our message is truth, and it works; the world's message is a mirage, and it destroys. Teenagers are intelligent enough to observe the clear evidence of that proposition and to tune their lives to its mandates.

## Getting Practical

Take a moment to consult your own recollections of adolescence. Do you remember when the subject of dating was mysterious and frightening? Sometimes we focus on the greater dangers and forget the simpler issues—the ones that are much closer and more tangible to our children. To a typical younger teen, sexuality is "way out there"—if you succeed in guidance—something not to be considered before marriage. But dating is another matter. Teenagers give a lot of thought to that particular social custom. They rehearse it in their minds, going over all the variables. It's something new and daunting.

When dating looms somewhere off on the horizon—say, when your teenager reaches age fourteen or so—you can begin to prepare her for the future. Help her understand that it's one more privilege to work toward. When she is mentally, spiritually, and emotionally ready, and given certain safe and appropriate conditions, she will be able to enjoy a date.

First, as I have mentioned, she will need to demonstrate how she handles herself in a group setting. This is one of the wonderful things about a church youth group: frequent, safe, nonpressured, and chaperoned opportunities for teenagers to "hang out." On a rafting trip, at a social, or even at a youth Bible study, teenagers can work on the special conditions of social dynamics. Again, you can probably remember the ups and downs, the little thrills and terrors of simply learning to be part of a group. What kinds of jokes go over well? When is it appropriate to speak up, and when should one remain silent? Teenagers figure out quickly that any group on any given date has its own distinct personality. There's plenty of emotional growth involved in simply learning these skills.

Talk to the youth leaders and ministry staff who see your teenager in these settings. How is she doing? Is she shy? Playful? Serious? Insensitive or awkward? Use your own experience to teach lessons such as how to use a sense of humor—teenagers depend a great deal on laughter and joking. Many teenagers use humor sarcastically and aggressively, not realizing that it hurts others and makes enemies. This is an opportunity for you to gently help your teen make a helpful adjustment.

Then, as the possibility of an actual date comes closer, spend time preparing your teenager based on what is appropriate for a boy or a girl. You'll find this to be greatly appreciated, as it takes much of the fear and awkwardness out of the experience. I took our Carey on a "test date" to show her what to expect. I showed how the young man may hold the car door open for her, may pull out her chair (or not). We talked about relaxing and chatting over dinner. Later, I talked with her about appropriate behavior on a date. On a first date, I pointed out, nothing more physical than, say, a slight touch on the arm or shoulder (say, at a movie) is really permissible. As time passes, and several dates have occurred between the same couple, there might be a peck on the cheek and ultimately a quick kiss on the lips, for example, or a short and innocent hug.

> **From the beginning, let your teenager know what is and is not appropriate and, of course, why.**

Such liberties must be earned with both time and the proof of maturity. But as I've stressed, teenagers understand boundaries and limitations—they simply want to know what they are. Most parents make the mistake of being far too vague, and this gives a kind of false license to overheated hormones sooner or later.

From the beginning, let your teenager know what is and is not appropriate and, of course, *why*. There should be guidelines for appropriate attire, because many teenagers dress suggestively these days, and that certainly compounds sexual temptation. Your teenager will understand that all these things—physical touch, clothing, absence of others—will raise the stakes and make the temptation stronger. Therefore I would emphasize a great deal of "group dating," chaperoned by trustworthy adults, at all stages of adolescence. Dating is a trust and a responsibility, like driving a car or (ultimately) being away at college. With more power comes more responsibility, and teenagers understand that these are not entitlements. They are prizes to be won through maturity and personal growth.

## A Teen's Declaration of Independence

Share these positive words with your teenager:

*Sexual purity means . . .*

- I have the *self-control* to manage my own actions.
- I have the *self-esteem* to overcome peer pressure.
- I have the *self-respect* to treat my body as God's temple.
- I have the *strength* to protect my future happiness.
- I have the *sincerity* to live out my personal beliefs.
- I have the *sensitivity* to respect the other person's feelings.
- I have the *sophistication* to see through the world's superficial values.

- I have the *security* to know I'm not at risk from STDs or pregnancy.
- I have the *satisfaction* of knowing that my decisions are pleasing to God.

## Help for Parents

Always remember that you, as a parent, have the greatest influence on your teenager. What you teach, through words and actions, will outweigh other teachings. But it's also important to think about the other influences that mold and shape a young mind—and how you can be certain they are working with you.

### Media

Please refer to Chapter 8, which is entirely devoted to this subject. We only want to emphasize that since we have a media-saturated culture—and since that media is saturated with sex—we need to be more than aware of the "teaching" that is going on. For example, research tells us that adolescents who watch a great deal of sex-related television are twice as likely as their peers who don't watch such television to begin engaging in sexual intercourse in the following year. That's according to a RAND report.[5] Rebecca Collins, a RAND psychologist who headed the study, said, "This is the strongest evidence yet that the sexual content of television programs encourages adolescents to initiate sexual intercourse and other sexual activities. The impact of television viewing is so large that even a moderate shift in the sexual content of adolescent TV watching could have a substantial effect on their sexual behavior."[6]

RAND also emphasizes that two-thirds of television entertainment programs contain sexual content, ranging from jokes and innuendo to intercourse and other behaviors.[7]

Given these facts, we cannot afford to be naive in allowing the television set to take over our homes. It's high time that parents went further than simply complaining about the content. We need to promote healthier alternatives or simply turn the set off. Even as parents make all the right moves in discussing the issues with their teenagers and presenting the biblical approaches, why allow that seductive electronic high-definition signal to undermine our messages?

## School

Are you aware of the sex education curriculum offered by your teenager's school? You're probably already aware that our public schools now generally assume that teenage sexual activity is normal and all but predestined. Therefore, their greatest emphasis is on the use of condoms as well as the prevention of sexually transmitted diseases and pregnancy. While we certainly want to educate our teenagers about these unwanted consequences, surely we must not assume that well-trained teenagers will engage in sexual activity no matter what, "because it is human nature." We want our teenagers to understand that because we respect them, we expect them to make wise decisions and restrain themselves from foolish behavior. Those

> Those who surrender to condom distribution are sending the message that teenagers are little more than animals who have no sense of judgment or self-control.

who surrender to condom distribution are sending the message that teenagers are little more than animals who have no sense of judgment or self-control.

Be certain you meet with the school officials and health faculty who are responsible for teaching sex education. Let them know your concerns and desires for the training of your own child. Be positive and friendly rather than threatening and defensive. If necessary, seek alternative educational arrangements for your teenager. But if he is progressing well in his mental, spiritual, and emotional training, you can help him think biblically about this and all other philosophies that are presented to him in school. He can understand that abstinence is not only the right spiritual approach, but the most practical and safe approach in these days of danger.

## Church

Many churches and Christian groups are responding to the sexual saturation of our children's world. Youth groups and Sunday school curricula are doing a much better job tackling sensitive issues directly. Church is another area that is assigned its own chapter in this book. But for now let's think a bit about how churches can support your training as a parent.

There are many fine examples of youth leaders doing creative and positive work. Writer Steve Rabey has profiled Tricia MacLeod, a Young Life leader in San Francisco who created a Valentine's weekend activity she called "Cupids on Ice," a weekend retreat for about fifty high school students and leaders. She brought in speakers recommended by the Bay Area Christian pregnancy center First Resort, which has done pioneering work in abstinence training.

The speakers addressed their topic with directness and from a teenager's point of view. They spoke realistically about drawing the lines and making future-driven decisions based on life goals. They dug into the Bible to learn its stances on sex, self-worth, repercussions, forgiveness, healing, and starting over. Testimonies were delivered by those with experiences to share so that the teenagers could evaluate real-life consequences in real witnesses.

"Instead of hammering the kids over the head," writes Rabey, "the speakers created an atmosphere where kids were able to be vulnerable and honest about their lives in small groups . . . There were many tears as kids worked through the pain in many areas of their lives."[8]

Think about your efforts toward training your teenager within the family context. Then imagine how effective it can be when your church is supporting you with creative and effective teaching, as well as surrounding your teenager with peers who are also seeking to please God in their youth.

## Gender Training

Finally, let's think about the place of gender. It's a more challenging subject than it's ever been in our world because there is much gender confusion, much discussion guided at eliminating the distinctions between the sexes.

We can applaud issues of fairness, such as equal pay for men and women in various jobs. But we need to help our teenagers understand that there are differences between men and women, and they are *built into* who we are. One of the first verses in our Bible reads, "So God created man in his own image, in the image of God he created him; male and female he created them" (Genesis

1:27). It is very clear from Scripture that part of the idea was for men and women to *complement* one another—to meet one another's needs, socially, physically, and emotionally. We are not only physically but also emotionally distinct. Masculinity and femininity are inborn traits that should not be glossed over or denied. "In the Lord, however, woman is not independent of man, nor is man independent of woman" (1 Corinthians 11:11). Our gender roles are something specially crafted by God, not something to be discarded. We need one another, and we need to value the differences in us that make each one special.

> **Every teenager needs a same-sex parent for a model.**

It's interesting that one consequence of today's gender confusion is an upswing in violence among adolescent girls. Joan Jacobs Brumberg, professor of history, human development, and gender studies at Cornell, says, "I don't want to blame women's liberation for violence among girls, but traditional femininity and passivity are no longer valued in young females."[9] *Newsweek* calls girl-on-girl violence a "burgeoning national crime."[10]

Every teenager needs a same-sex parent for a model. Boys look to fathers and girls look to mothers for specific training in their gender roles. We have more single parents than ever before, of course, and that brings special challenges. If you are a single mother with a son, for instance, the father is hopefully still available to his son. If not, is there an uncle or a grandfather or a close (and trustworthy) male friend who would spend special time with your son?

Only an older male can be a mentor in masculinity, and only an older female can be a mentor in femininity. Part of this task is to teach a teenager his or her proper relationship to, and respect for, the opposite sex. The New Testament teaching is not for men to "rule" women oppressively, but to reserve a special reverence and esteem for them. "The woman is the glory of man" (1 Corinthians 11:7). In raising our sons, I gave special attention to seeing that they respected the opposite sex in a special way. We taught them all the traditional manners—holding open the door of a restaurant or a church, for instance, and allowing the woman to pass through first. They found, of course, that women appreciate that level of etiquette.

Pat worked, in turn, to help Carey learn the subtleties of femininity that men appreciate—not being loud or aggressive but being gentle and warm. Teenagers must be taught that much of pop culture's treatment of gender is dehumanizing, reducing either sex to a mindless object of physical lust. We hear a lot about secular humanism, but this is *de*-humanism—and young people will take the point seriously when we show it to them.

A few days ago I met a nice young lady with her nose in a book at Starbucks. I asked her what she was reading and she replied, "Well, the title is kind of embarrassing. But it's a wonderful book! She showed me the cover: *Boys Will Put You on a Pedestal (So They Can Look Up Your Skirt): A Dad's Advice for Daughters*, by Philip Van Munching (I suppose the author was accustomed to having an interesting name himself, so he gave one to his book). The young lady began telling me all the things she was learning from the book and how she wished her dad had said these things to her.

My curiosity was piqued, so I went into a bookstore and picked up "the pedestal book." She was right. This is one of the best little parenting books I've ever seen, and I've bought several copies to give away. While Van Munching's work isn't necessarily written from a spiritual perspective, he hits all the right notes, speaking directly to his daughter with humor, love, and real understanding. He includes chapters on beauty, boyfriends, the Internet, cynicism (what a great subject for teenagers), tattoos, vulgarity, and many other topics. But he masters the challenge of talking *with* instead of *at* a teenage girl.

I mention this book not only because I highly recommend it, but because I wanted to quote the chapter on abstinence and sexual purity:

> Doing it so that a boy will love you . . . or even "like" you . . . is cheating yourself in a dozen different ways. First off, it never works: if the goal of the boy is to have sex, the relationship is effectively over as soon as you've done it. Sure, he might stick around to "score" a few times, but the thrill of that wears off. And when it does, he's gone . . . Here's something else that's not fair: when they're looking for serious relationships, boys avoid girls who are thought of as [promiscuous]. Those girls seem somehow "dirty" to them. Used.[11]

I would recommend that dads (moms too) read this book together. If nothing else, it will break the ice on honest issues about growing up to be a young woman of integrity in this modern world.

The topics of gender and sexuality can be challenging, can't they? I hope you'll teach these lessons positively in your home, for what could be a more joyful subject? Past generations made the mistake of associating sexuality with wickedness and ugliness. These matters weren't to be discussed at all. The predictable result was that young people developed psychological, physical, and social problems of all kinds that were connected to sexuality. The current generation, of course, has made just the opposite mistake. Neither is the right path. Instead, let's begin with a biblical foundation, understanding the role of male and female in creation, as sanctioned by God.

Let's help our children understand that sexual intimacy within marriage is a sacred and wonderful gift. If you train your teenager with love and patience, in the context of God's guidance, you need never have anxiety about this subject. It need not be the weapon of a morally bankrupt society, but one more window to understand the goodness of our Lord.

# 10

# teaching values

YOUR SON IS SITTING IN A WARM CLASSROOM IN LATE MAY. HIS Algebra 2 final exam is on his desk, and he has a very bad feeling about it.

It's not as if he didn't prepare. He studied all week, even drilled for hours with his older brother. But there's just so much pressure. The question of college is always in the back of his mind. If he's going to win enrollment, he'll need some financial scholarship help. That means he needs to "ace" this course as well as his units of science, history, language arts, and the rest. But good grief, this exam is more difficult than he ever imagined.

The quadratic equation at the top of the third page is making no sense. Your son stops to take a deep breath and clear his mind. As he glances upward, his eyes light on Jennie, a classmate who sits just in front and to the left. She's a well-established, certified

"AlgeBrain," and it's obvious that she's cruising through the test like a sharp blade through melted butter. She always does. She has probably already solved this quadratic equation.

Your son swallows nervously. His eyes linger on Jennie's hyperactive pencil. The girl's in such a "zone" that she's oblivious to her classmates, making no attempt to conceal her work. One quick glance, and no one would know. It may be the boost he needs toward an A, toward college, toward making Mom and Dad happy . . .

Just behind your son sits his best friend, Eric. Eric has been struggling with the test himself and happens to have gazed upward at the same time. His eyes light on your son and follow his glance to Jennie the AlgeBrain. These two boys are good friends who know each other well. Eric senses the pressure on your son's shoulders. He knows how difficult this Algebra 2 course has been. It takes no rocket scientist to figure out what idea is going through your son's mind right now. With a twinge of panic, Eric wonders what he should do in case that particular development occurs right in front of him. Like the other students, he has signed a school honor code. He has affixed his signature to a solemn vow that he will report any cheating he may observe.

But this is his best friend! He can't possibly be expected to damage his friend's future by reporting him on the final exam. Maybe he should just look down and mind his own business. What he doesn't see, he can't report. Eric feels sick to his stomach. It is very difficult for him to refocus on his own examination . . .

Meanwhile, there is Jennie, noted math whiz, her pencil winding through the obstacles on her examination. She knows nothing of the rumbling clouds of anxiety behind her—but she has more than enough of her own. Even as she dispatches problem 43, her mind is on . . . *automobiles.*

Jennie cannot stop thinking about her mother's car, which she drove to school yesterday. It was so nice to be allowed to drive to her classes. After school, she stopped at the convenience store to pick up a soft drink. But as she was pulling back out of the lot, she scraped the shiny silver Lexus parked next to her. There didn't seem to be any damage at all to her mother's car, but the Lexus definitely was a bit creased and crumpled. Jennie panicked and stepped on the accelerator, vacating the premises in twin puffs of exhaust and burnt rubber. If her parents found out about this, she could lose all her driving privileges. She would probably be forced to take an after-school job to pay for the damage. Yet her parents expect a perfect report card, don't they? They *demand* it, actually. An afternoon job at the food court would make that impossible. Surely the Lexus was insured—anyone with such an expensive ride could afford to fix it anyway. It's a lesser-of-two-evils thing, isn't it? It's got to be.

Then why isn't her conscience giving her a moment's peace? The lone pearl of a tear begins its southward course as Jennie turns to the fourth page.

Three teens, three moments of truth—character-molding moments that may reflect all the guidance, wisdom, and preparation we have poured into parenting. How would your teenager handle such crises?

Some principles are easy to teach. It's not difficult to train a little one not to touch a hot stove, for the consequences are as memorable as a burnt finger. That kind of lesson teaches itself. For that matter, most parents easily teach counting, spelling, telling time, tying shoes. But when we enter the moral and ethical realm,

> **When we enter the moral and ethical realm, that's when the issue of character really looms before us.**

that's when the issue of character really looms before us. The lesson doesn't teach itself quite so clearly, does it?

To touch a hot stove brings pain, but to cheat on a test brings a better grade, better prospects, and happier parents. The consequences are real enough, but not so immediate or tangible. We need more wisdom and finesse to show our children the true implications that lie between honor and dishonor; that honesty is not the best but the *only* policy; that a person's name is a precious commodity that must be protected through a life of integrity; and that, yes, there *is* a hot-stove effect, sooner or later, on the far side of cheating.

You and I understand the pain that results when we step outside the boundaries laid out by parents, teachers, church, society, and God. It has been said that we do not so much break God's laws as break ourselves upon them. We must find a way to help our teenagers see the undeniable truth of life's demand for unassailable character, values, and integrity.

## The Value of Values

Since we've already raised the question of cheating in school, let's look at a snapshot of modern attitudes in the high school classroom. In a recent survey, 84 percent of high school students judged cheating to be "common" among their peers. Seventy-eight percent of them admitted they themselves had cheated, and 95 percent of those who cheated said they did not get caught.[1]

Now compare those figures with the results of the same questions some sixty years ago, when only 20 percent admitted to having cheated in high school. The numbers have nearly reversed themselves, as 22 percent today report they do not cheat.[2] Donald McCabe of Rutgers University has conducted his own research into cheating with similar results. When he asked his student respondents why they cheated, he often heard about academic pressure. But most students pointed to poor examples set by the world at large. To compound the problem, McCabe discovered that faculty members were usually aware of cheating in their classrooms but often decided to do nothing about it.[3]

Still, other research comes from the Josephson Institute of Ethics, which observes that though one in four teenagers have shoplifted within one year, the same young people perceive themselves as having strong character. Why? The institute points to "high levels of cynicism" among our current young people—particularly among males. They see the world as a place where one might as well steal.[4]

Once again, this is what teenagers are learning from the world. Nearly half of them believed that though it was wrong to cheat, it was often necessary. Teenagers are being driven by higher demands, with rising college costs and more pervasive images of financial success. At the same time, they are observing presidents who commit adultery and lie under oath; athletes who cheat by using steroids; celebrities who hire high-profile lawyers and escape punishment; and a general vacuum of heroes and role models.

The question must be asked: Has human nature changed? Have we simply harvested a poor crop of teenagers? Of course not. Young people continue to look to their parents and adult mentors. They are still teachable, trainable, and, as a matter of fact, remarkably promising in many respects. This generation is one that is concerned about truth and ultimate values. Our young people are interested in examining questions of ethics and morals and eager to escape hypocrisy and superficiality. What they need is parents who will help them understand that integrity and morality are not only still possible—but that any other road leads to self-destruction.

> **The home needs to be a positive place undergirded by positive values.**

Solomon, the wisest man of his age, spoke for us all: "Listen, my son, to your father's instruction and do not forsake your mother's teaching. They will be a garland to grace your head and a chain to adorn your neck" (Proverbs 1:8–9). Our goal is for our children to put such a high value on the training they receive. In ancient literature the garland and chain were marks of attainment, wisdom, and high position in society. Many young people today believe that material prizes, not training, bring rewards of that type. We want them to value the wisdom we have for them. Let's discuss some of the best methods for guiding our teenagers spiritually.

## The Positive Household

I believe the home needs to be a positive place undergirded by positive values. That seems to be an obvious assertion, but look at so many of the homes around us. What attitudes toward the world do our teenagers absorb? All too easily our children pick up despair, cynicism, and a negative spirit. I'm certain that few if any parents realize they are passing on such a legacy. But it's quite important that you stop and examine your family dynamics carefully. Consider what attitudes the children in your home encounter when it comes to:

- Your job or your spouse's job.
- Your neighbors.
- Fellow church members and leaders.
- In-laws and extended family members.
- Political figures and parties.

The truth is that positive young people cannot be raised by negative parents. A dark spirit permeates a home and everyone in it. Here are the elements your teenagers crave:

- *Hope* for a brighter future.
- *Challenge* to become more skilled, more intelligent, and more effective.
- *Encouragement*, one to another, as we press on toward our goals.

This doesn't mean a naive, Pollyanna-type approach to life. We acknowledge that the world can be a hopeless place, but because of God and our love for one another, there is hope to be found. We recognize the problems among our leaders, our culture, even our churches—but we are convinced that we can be part of the solution rather than part of the problem. Teenagers need to see excited, energized parents who are pursuing their own roles in life with the same kind of attitudes they expect their children to take to school. If Dad is constantly saying something negative about the boss or the organization, he can expect his children to begin viewing their own world in the same light. On the other hand, think of the most positive families you have known. You will find that their enthusiasm radiates through their children and out into their world. Enthusiasm becomes a legacy that does not fade with time.

In Bible times Hebrew mothers and fathers aligned their homes by this declaration from God:

> Fix these words of mine in your hearts and minds; tie them as symbols on your hands and bind them on your foreheads. Teach them to your children, talking about them when you sit at home and when you walk along the road, when you lie down and when you get up. Write them on the doorframes of your houses and on your gates, so that your days and the days of your children may be many in the land that the LORD swore to give your forefathers, as many as the days that the heavens are above the earth. (Deuteronomy 11:18–21)

Notice the wisdom that comes through those lines:

- God's wisdom should be engraved mentally and spiritually in our families.
- God's wisdom should be visible on our hands (work) and faces (attitudes).
- God's wisdom should be taught to children every single moment, dawn to dusk.
- God's wisdom should be carved upon our front and back doors (dealings with the world).
- God's wisdom creates a legacy of joy that transcends time and space.

Those are powerful, life-transforming, family-enhancing thoughts. The spiritual training in your home is set in terms of the *absolute*: always teaching at all levels, in all activities, at all places, and at all times. The demands are matched only by the reward, which is nothing less than an eternal blessing that brings a little of heaven to earth.

> **If your teenager feels well loved, he will follow your lead as you guide him spiritually.**

But this means as parents we must devote ourselves wholly and utterly to creating a home that immerses our children in spiritual values. It means parents must look first to their own hearts, their own hands, their own standards. This is demanding, but it's worth the effort for you and the future of your blessed children.

Remember, too, that the most foundational task for a parent at this and every stage is to provide unconditional love and to keep the emotional tank filled. If your teenager feels well loved, he will follow your lead as you guide him spiritually in all the ways detailed above. If he does not, you won't be successful in your training. So begin with love and be conscious of every opportunity to shape and mold the heart, mind, and spirit of your teenager.

As we explore how you can do that, let's learn a bit more about how the teenage mind develops.

## Wired for Sound Values

New and groundbreaking revelations about the adolescent mind have come in our age. As we've seen earlier, the conventional wisdom about cognitive development has changed a great deal. It was once assumed that one's basic core personality and behavior patterns were set at an early age. But that's not the case at all. We know that your child experienced a virtual explosion of learning in the first ten years of life. But it's also true that a crucial period of personality determination comes during early adolescence.

All the basic "wiring" has been laid down during those early years, yet the young person still has a great range of possibilities in terms of future development. In early adolescence he begins to gain the ability to think abstractly—in practical terms, to question what is right or wrong. He becomes much more aware of inconsistencies in his world. Still, there is a great deal of immaturity and impulsive reasoning. During the middle teenage years, the young person begins to truly understand two points of view, though he may still be stubborn about his own stance. It's a matter of emotional maturity. Finally, in later adolescence, your teenager will have a much stronger ability to empathize—to see an issue from multiple perspectives. If you have some difference of opinion with him, he is more likely to understand and dignify your side of things, while holding to his own determination.

What is happening inside? We don't want to reduce the human soul to a network of electrical wiring, but our thinking does move through neural connections known as synapses. In studying the progress of this interior wiring system, we have seen how the teenage mind develops. The period of adolescence will arrange the wiring in a manner that will serve the person for the rest of his life. To explain it another way, the teenager establishes certain habits and behavior patterns during this critical time. Other habits and other behaviors are left behind. The active ones become strong and fairly permanent, while the neglected ones slowly fade. Can you see the implication? If your teenager's life is filled with good, wholesome activities and learning experiences; if he is developing his gifts and talents; if his spirit is under wise guidance—then those behaviors will be set for many years to come.

This poses a few questions for the wise parent. Is your teenager getting the right amount of exercise, developing good study habits, or spending too much time staring passively at a television or computer screen? The use of time at this stage has a kind of double value. It has value now and even more value later. If we begin with the end in mind, we should begin training our teenagers with an eye toward the young adults we want them to become.

## Your Example

The disciples, probably not much older than teenagers themselves, clustered about Jesus and begged, "Teach us to pray, just as John taught his disciples" (Luke 11:1). They, too, lived in a disrupted, culturally chaotic world. They saw a group of younger people (the followers of John the Baptist) who seemed to have some direction, some vision. I believe our young people today are requesting the same of us. *Teach us to pray. Show us how to connect with God. Give us some foundation to cling to when there is so much confusion.*

Certainly you desire that your teenager adopts your faith for his own. He will actually look to you, the parent, for faith and slavation issues more than you may realize. He might look beyond the talk and the formalities and wonder, *Is God a concept or a real, living guide? Is he a "bogeyman" created to instill fear, or is he a Father who is love's fullest expression?*

Does your teen ever see you pray? Does he ever see you use the Bible to make a decision? Do you discuss favorite insights from the sermon on the way to Sunday dinner, or is it all about the day's NFL football game?

Stop and try to remember the last true family crisis—a lost job, or a dying relative perhaps. Did God figure into the situation around your home? Did your teenager see spiritual maturity or helpless fear?

The song could be talking about our teenagers when it says, "They will know we are Christians by our love." As John the Apostle wrote, "Whoever does not love does not know God, because God is love" (1 John 4:8). This is exactly how young people look at us. How do we talk about the boss at work? The rude neighbor? How do we behave in a tense traffic jam? It's difficult to know we are being watched all the time, but our teenagers are certainly doing that. They have heard that God is love, and they want to see if that has any effect on the way we behave. Does your teenager see love in your relationships?

> **Does your teen ever see you pray? Does he ever see you use the Bible to make a decision?**

Here's an important question: Does your teen experience the joy of your salvation? If the spiritual life in our homes and our churches were truly joyful and truly dynamic, and if we the parents were truly committed to it, then I don't believe there would be any mass exodus of young people from the church. If they had learned to let their faith bring them great contentment in life, why would they ever abandon it?

Consider a family devotional time. If you can't make it happen every evening, then once a week would be a great deal better than never. If that's impossible, once a month would still be better than what most families manage. Have an enjoyable time of sharing and prayer, with lots of laughter and honesty. Pray for one another. Challenge one another to let God be a bigger part of the following day. For example, you might say, "Tomorrow, let's each ask the Lord to show us someone for whom we can do a good deed. Then, tomorrow night we can compare notes and see how good it made each of us feel."

Even at unexpected times you can create a spiritual moment in your family. After watching a movie together on TV, turn off the set and prompt a discussion about the message in the movie. How does it relate to the Christian faith? What might Jesus have done in the situation you've just seen?

Then, let your teenager know you're praying for him every single day. Write a note saying this and leave it in his textbook or lunch sack. Mention a specific victory you're praying for on his behalf, then ask for updates to see how God answered the prayer. I can't overemphasize the impact of spiritual leadership on your teenager—even just a little bit of it. It can make a profound difference in this crucial adolescent phase when the wiring is being laid inside, and the thoughts and habits of the moment can become the patterns of a lifetime.

## The Place of Church

As we close this chapter, let's think together about one of the most essential aspects of nurturing the teenage soul. The Bible offers us no option for spiritual growth aside from committed fellowship. God wants our lives involved in the church and the church involved in our lives. "Now you are the body of Christ, and each one of you is a part of it" (1 Corinthians 12:27). I can't imagine anyone being a lackluster church member and expecting their children to end up with strong faith.

But today there is reason for great concern about the future of our young people and church. Tom Elliff, chairman of the Southern Baptist Convention's Council on Family Life, announced the results of a study that rocked the Christian world. The council found that 88 percent of evangelical children leave church around the age of eighteen, never to return.[5]

Meanwhile, pollster George Barna examines his own troubling findings. He believes that younger people drop out of church because they struggle to find a place there. He points out that they are one-third less likely than older adults to attend, give financially, or read the Bible. Barna is most concerned about the 58 percent decline in attendance among eighteen- to twenty-nine-year-olds who were faithful churchgoers in their teens. He blames the decline on younger people's quest for personal fulfillment and the tendency of churches to overlook young leaders.[6]

But wait—isn't it true that young people naturally drop out of church? They get married, get busy with their careers, build their cocoons, then return to the home church and ask for help with their own kids. If we raise them right, they come back as surely as the blooms in springtime, don't they? Perhaps so, to some small extent. But all time periods are not created equally; we are no longer living in the 1950s or 1960s, when life was relatively simpler and our culture was more cohesive. The findings of Barna and others are quite disturbing, for it

> The church must "build a better mousetrap."

appears that, despite efforts to contemporize our worship, we are losing the wider battle for the souls of our young people.

What the church can do to remedy this is a subject for another book. Obviously, among other things, the church must "build a better mousetrap." It must have more relevant ministries, and it must create leadership opportunities that young adults can latch on to. But what can you as a parent do to make the church experience more effective and lasting for your teenager? I suggest several considerations:

## Model Good Churchmanship and Attendance

The point is obvious, but it cannot be overlooked. Adults who attended church regularly as a child are nearly three times as likely to be attending a church today as are their peers who avoided the church during childhood (61 percent to 22 percent, respectively).[7] If you attend sporadically, you are teaching your teenager that the church is sporadically worthwhile. "Let us not give up meeting together, as some are in the habit of doing, but let us encourage one another" (Hebrews 10:25). If you avoid volunteering for committees and Sunday school leadership, your teenager takes in that message as well. And if you practice "serial churchmanship," attending whatever fellowship has the most attractive program from week to week, again there is a harmful message.

I strongly recommend that you make sure you're in a powerful, vibrant church that has good programs for every member of your family. Also, offer yourself faithfully and consistently to use your spiritual gifts toward the unity and growth of that church. You need not attend every single service or program—some families actually do this to the detriment of their own home relationships. But the church should be a central, unifying element for your family. It's one of the last institutions where families can sit together, participate together, and have a long-term commitment that will one day be treasured by our grown children. In raising teenagers, the church is your friend—one of the best and only ones, for that matter. For that reason, it's worth making a few sacrifices: perhaps not spending every possible weekend at the summer lake house, for example. Ultimately, we understand that Christ gave his life, the ultimate sacrifice, for the church. Surely it's worth any lesser sacrifice we can make, especially knowing all the good things that come back to us and our children in return.

### Get Behind the Pastor

I know and support many ministers who have been substantially abused by their congregations. It's the dark underside of American church life, and it has grown to be an epidemic in recent years. Many of our churches are constantly embattled by divisions and pew uprisings, and there is no way we can create a healthy environment for our impressionable teenagers under these circumstances. At the same time, if you gossip about the leadership at home, you are reinforcing antiauthority attitudes in your children. Remember that the pastor has a position of great sacrifice and tremendous difficulty. The greatest contribution you can make to your church is to be a peacemaker. "Make every effort to keep the unity of the Spirit through the bond of peace" (Ephesians 4:3).

### Get Close to the Youth Pastor

If there is any job more difficult than that of the pastor, it is that of the youth pastor. Here are servants called to lead the most challenging age-group—while being extremely young themselves!

Youth leaders rarely last long because their responsibility is so grueling, and they receive so little support. I've observed parents making excessive demands of these overburdened, often undertrained leaders. They want the youth pastor to solve all the problems created by poor parenting and to miraculously transform their teenagers into all-American, problem-free young people. Let me offer you one powerful tip: if you invest yourself in making the youth pastor your friend, your teenager will reap the dividends. Simply offering encouragement and emotional support will be profoundly appreciated and reflected in service to your teenager. Open your home to youth activities, and volunteer to help drive or chaperone when it is needed. If you want the church to be a place your teenagers love and respect, do more than your share to help make it so.

## Look for Joyful Leadership

Particularly in decades past, Sunday school could actually be a daunting place for young people. A young lady stood up in her classroom and, with great passion, described a doubt she was experiencing about God and his love. The teacher scolded and warned her: questions like that one could lead to judgment from God! The young lady ran from the classroom in tears and refused to set foot in church for many years afterward.

Church should be a place of joy and celebration. It should also be a place where the Bible is taught, where serious issues are taught, and where doubts can be freely shared. Otherwise, our teenagers will brand church as just another place where adult hypocrisy rules the day. Take a close look at the adults who will be working with your teenager. Why not get involved yourself so you can be close at hand? If your teenager loves church and finds that it responds to his deepest questions and needs, you won't find yourself wondering whether he'll leave never to return. Instead, you'll find him inviting his friends.

**Church should be a place of joy and celebration.**

I hope you will daily be aware of the importance of spiritual growth in your teenager. Some parents spend a great deal of money to send their children to tennis camps or private schools, yet spend few moments talking together about spiritual things. Jesus cut to the very heart of the matter when he said, "For where your treasure is, there your heart will be also" (Luke 12:34). No treasure is greater than our children—except for Christ himself. Let's be absolutely certain that we bring those two together.

# 11

# anxiety, depression, and other challenges

I T's ALL PSYCHOBABBLE," SAYS DAD WITH A DISMISSIVE WAVE OF his hand. Mom has just come home from the doctor with Emily, their daughter. "Emily doesn't have some fancy *disorder*. She's a just an ordinary kid. All she needs to do is eat regularly—three square meals—and everything will be fine."

Sometimes parents have trouble accepting the reality of a behavior with a "fancy" name. For one thing, we all want to believe the very best about our children. And many moms and dads aren't predisposed to accepting newer understandings of behavior that weren't around when they were young. It's easy to suspect that somehow our culture has invented all these maladies. But there can be little doubt that behavioral disorders have always been around. We have just come to recognize them more clearly, and for the first time we've given some of them names. It's now possible to read back through history and spot the unmistakable signs of ADHD, for example, in certain famous men and women.

For another thing, it's possible that we see more problematic behavior symptoms in our young people today because there is so much fear, so much anxiety, and so much depression in our world. There is simply more stress and more tension in the world of the average teenager.

> **There is simply more stress and more tension in the world of the average teenager.**

There are many reasons for this, but whatever they may be, it's most important that every parent be aware of danger signals and resources for treatment. There should be no stigma in the diagnosis of a special challenge, whether it's a learning disability or an eating disorder or some other issue. These are all symptoms of being human in an inhuman world. Each of us has known our share of fear, anxiety, and depression.

We parents can also remember how our own emotions were powerfully intensified during the period of adolescence. There is no other time like it in the human life span, and there has been no other time like today in history. The kinds of challenges discussed in this chapter are the result. Hopefully you will receive information here that may allow you to be informed and prepared before any crisis arrives. Know, too, it could be that your child, well loved and well trained in managing anger, will not be troubled by any of these phenomena.

But even if you're doing a wonderful job as a parent, life is life. Conditions are imperfect. Sometimes the life path becomes rocky.

Let's take a look at the special challenges and special needs of teenagers.

## Helping Teenagers with Fear and Anxiety

What worries teenagers?

- They fear terrorism and nuclear war.
- They fear an outbreak of violence at school.
- They fear the attention of relentless bullies.
- They fear teachers, principals, and those who hold power over them.
- They fear the irresistible suction of peer pressure.
- They fear the loss of a parent.
- They fear the loss of childhood and the demands of growing up.
- They fear they won't measure up socially.
- They fear that their secret thoughts mean they're abnormal.
- They fear unpredictable surges of adolescent emotion.
- They fear the possibility of dying overseas in a war.

The list could stretch on. Fear is a by-product of change, and change is just part of life. But there are more changes during these years of adolescence, perhaps, than at any other time of life. A teenager is pushed from the comfort zone, a secure world of parental protection, into a place where she herself must begin to make her own decisions and look out for herself. The teenager has an expanded version of a child's imagination, but a more adult perspective of the true dangers all around us. That's an uncomfortable combination.

On top of that, consider it's a world of traumatic change for all of us. There is less permanence than ever to which we can cling. We have our own anxieties, but imagine coping with such changes in the outside world while there are even greater changes going on inside. That's the world your teenager must confront, and a certain amount of fear is simply inevitable. But what can you do? Your teenager may be very hesitant to verbalize her fears. In her world it's considered cool to face everything with a shrug and a wry put-down. Friends might laugh if she put words to her feelings—so she doesn't, even with you.

We'll discuss your best strategy for helping her. But first, consider the place of anxiety.

## Stress and Anxiety

Anxiety is complex; a good emotion with ill effects. After all, anxiety ties us in knots inside. It increases the blood pressure, even causes feelings of panic in some cases. You feel anxiety when your teenager takes that car out for the first lone journey around the block. It's an emotion that says we care. We all experience this protective instinct that starts the day our baby is born and never stops.

But anxiety can enslave us. It is fear coiled around us so that we are never free from its pressure. And much of the time we may not even be certain what we're anxious about. The word *stress* is used more and more often for anxiety. It is usually described as a mental or emotional strain set off by change. We might think of a fear as having an identifiable cause, such as any of those on the list above. Anxiety is something more elusive, something more comprehensive. There are times when we lie awake and can't quickly isolate the source of our discomfort. That's how anxiety works.

I've always found great comfort in facing my own anxieties with this passage from Paul—a man, by the way, who wrote from prison where he faced execution:

> Do not be anxious about anything, but in everything, by prayer and petition, with thanksgiving, present your requests to God. And the peace of God, which transcends all understanding, will guard your hearts and your minds in Christ Jesus. (Philippians 4:6–7)

We have God's promise that we can bring our anxiety to him, and he will bring his peace to us. Just knowing that brings a great deal of reassurance.

And yes, we're discussing *your* fear and anxiety as well as that of your teenager. Remember that both of these emotions are contagious. If you're always a little jittery, you can be certain your jitteriness is going to wear off on your teenager. So the first thing you need to do is come to grips with your own stress, fear, and anxiety. Give it wholly to God. Discuss it with your spouse and your closest friends. Remember that your teenager has her own personal "worry closet"—as well as the overflow from yours. Loving her as you do, you want her to be as free as possible from negative emotions.

> We have God's promise that we can bring our anxiety to him, and he will bring his peace to us.

Is your teenager suffering from fear and/or anxiety? Even if she isn't bringing her worries to you, be vigilant. Keep your eyes and ears open, as well as operating that intuitive parental antenna.

Pay attention to how well your teenager is sleeping. Is she tossing and turning, getting up a lot at night? Does she seem even more tired in the morning?

Listen to her tone of voice at the times she does speak. What is her attitude about life in general? About her friends? About school, church, hobbies? She may not verbalize her anxiety—she may not know how to, or what it's all about—but she will drop clues, her way of saying, "All is not right with me. Can you help?"

## Your Best Approach

It should come as no surprise to learn that the best thing you can do for your teenager is to keep the emotional tank filled. It makes all the difference. Fear and anxiety have a lot to do with the basic need for security. So many teenagers feel insecure.

Therefore, provide all the love your child needs. Reinforce the idea that she will be accepted and cared for no matter what. Even when she feels ugly, her face has acne, she is coping with the new challenge of menstrual cycles, her moods aren't too attractive—no matter what, she cannot lose your love. Unconditional love dissolves a good bit of powerful anxiety. John makes the point for us in his epistle: "There is no fear in love. But perfect love drives out fear, because fear has to do with punishment. The one who fears is not made perfect in love" (1 John 4:18).

Consider, too, the alternatives. The child who does not receive unconditional love will not develop the compassion that makes up positive anxiety. She will not learn to care deeply for others because she will not have experienced that care herself.

Provide the basic love. Fill the tank. Model for her the very best way to handle difficult emotions. And of course, be ready to listen. It's all right to ask light, nonpressuring questions: "Tough day?" Be as available as possible so that when she is ready to bring you her whole tangled mess of negative emotions, you'll be ready to listen and guide her.

On those occasions, please don't try to fix everything too easily! Remember that there are times when the greatest need is simply to be heard and understood; to gain a bit of empathy. Ask leading questions, such as, "How does that make you feel?" Let her talk as much as she wants, and as freely as she wants, about her fears and anxieties, even though you may be tempted to jump in with quick solutions.

Finally, there will be an opportunity to help find positive answers and reasons for reassurance. You will be surprised at how often she will provide these herself. After all, you've been helping her "think out loud," and it's important that she learn to work through crises on her own. This is a key part of the process of maturation. If she is anxious about an allegedly cruel, sadistic new chemistry teacher, ask her what she thinks are some sensible ways to approach the problem.

And there will be some tougher issues requiring good parental advice. What about bullies? What about peer pressure to drink? You can help her find the resources to confront bigger problems.

Finally, watch out for the possible result of fear and anxiety: depression. This is a topic every parent must consider carefully, so let's explore it closely.

## Depression and Teenagers

Experts agree that one in eight teenagers may suffer from depression. They also agree that most parents are missing the signals.

This means that their children are not receiving serious assistance.[1] Therefore, it may be that your son or daughter faces the challenge of clinical depression, but you have the choice of being better informed so that your child can receive the appropriate care.

Depression on an epic scale is a symptom of our times. There has been a great shift in generational awareness and reporting of the phenomenon. Ronald Kessler of Harvard Medical School studied eight thousand Americans ages fifteen to fifty-four. Of those now forty-five to fifty-four, only 2 percent reported symptoms of depression by their late teens. But in the age range of fifteen to twenty-four, 23 percent reported serious depression before age twenty.[2] Today, nearly everyone knows of the close association between adolescence and depression.

Depression isn't a grumpy mood that passes. It's no small problem, and something more is called for than "putting on a happy face." We know that younger people who develop depression or anxiety are three to four times more likely than their peers to have drug or alcohol abuse problems by their mid-twenties. Depression has strong connections to the epidemic of teenage suicide that has flared in recent years. Between 1950 and 1995, suicide rates for children and teens quadrupled.

> **One in eight teenagers may suffer from depression.**

Severe anxiety is the most frequent catalyst of teenage depression. Depressed teens are nearly always anxiety-driven, and this is true of adolescents from every background, rich or poor, rural or urban.

We can make further points about depressed children:

- They tend to come from homes of either divorce or heightened tension.
- They seem to be socially less adept; they either receive or imagine rejection, and are therefore shy and withdrawn.
- They suffer from poor self-image, connecting their problems to perceived personal flaws—as opposed to changeable behavior.
- They experience large loads of stress.
- They suffer from shorter attention spans and struggle to complete goals.

Boys deal with depression too. The problem is, we find out about it even more rarely in their case. Boys deal with their depression through action rather than passivity. They may pick fights; they may steal or lie or drive a car at a dangerous speed.

We see depression in girls primarily after the age of eleven. Over the next four years, we are far more likely to see it arise. At eighteen girls have twice the rate of depression that boys have. Like adult women, girls tend to dwell more on problems than males; therefore, they slide more easily into negative mind-sets. As nurturers, they suffer more from worry and anxiety. And in the teenage years they find many objects for anxiety: appearance, family problems, and popularity, for example. We tend to train our girls to be caring in orientation. Again, it's a blade that cuts both ways—they have deeper sensitivities, and in turn they can suffer from them.

## Identifying Depression

Depression can hide beneath is own symptoms. For example, you would be immediately alarmed by the discovery that your teenager was abusing drugs, and you might miss the fact that it was actually a symptom of a more complex emotional depression.

We have discovered that depression comes on very subtly, slowly, and gradually in younger people. There is a certain interplay between the main problem and its symptoms, in that they aggravate one another. If your child's grades drop off in school, you might try many responses before considering the possibility of depression. You might make the mistake of focusing on the surface problem, because again, no parent wants his or her child to struggle in school. But you will attack the problem in vain unless you deal with the root cause.

But don't forget the complexity of this problem. For example, there may be neurological factors in your teenager's grade problems, but they may be aggravated by the depression.

You would be more likely to recognize depression in yourself; adults are more emotionally articulate and subtle in their understanding. But teenagers are confused. They may be vaguely aware that something is wrong, but they don't know what it is.

In this particularly negative and often distressing world, we need to do what we can to be certain a teenager lives in a positive and emotionally nourishing environment. There is a very dark culture of music, movies, games, Web sites, and ideas for teenagers today. Many of them are attracted to *darkness* in tone. Therefore, do what you can to keep your teenager around positive and healthy influences—the kind a church youth group or athletic team is likely to offer. As a matter of fact, sports and physical exertion can be a very positive and cathartic outlet for teenage depression.

## Telltale Signs

If your teenager displays not one but *several* of these symptoms, you should consider consultation and counseling.

- Feelings of sadness, hopelessness, despair; lack of purpose or lack of interest in activities that have brought pleasure in the past
- Short attention span and an inability to concentrate or make a decision
- Inattention to personal hygiene
- The decision to quit Scouts, clubs, youth group, team sports, music, etc.
- A rapid plummet in academic performance
- Extreme amounts of time spent alone
- Physical symptoms: persistent aching, either muscular or common headaches; lack of energy; a rapid increase or decrease in appetite; weight changes; inability to sleep, or the desire to sleep too often
- Unpredictable moods: irritability, anxiety, surly disposition, or frequent disputes with others.

You may want to talk to your child's teachers, coaches, and youth leaders. Have they noticed behavioral changes?

Remember, it's often a gray issue rather than one of black and white. For example, most teenagers close their bedroom doors and ask to spend time alone. A headache could be a sinus problem rather than one of depression. What you're on the lookout for is a *grouping* of some of these symptoms—and of course, parental intuition that there is something deeply worrying your teenager.

## Acting It Out

If we don't intervene, then, as the saying goes, "something's gotta give." The teenager will finally have to act on the outside in response to the turbulence on the inside. These actions can come in many forms.

In general, boys are more likely to act out their depression through violence. Our culture has traditionally socialized them to be aggressive and active rather than reflective. In particular, we are seeing the behavior of breaking and entering among boys. Why would a depressed teenage boy do such a thing? It provides excitement, the thrill of something forbidden, that could break through the pain and the gloom. It's also aggressive—a form of striking back at the world. What happens when the intruder is apprehended? Agencies, the police, and parents will deal with the behavior rather than the symptom.

For girls, we are seeing a trend toward sexual promiscuity as a way of handling depression. Again, it is a rebellious way to gain a quick, adrenaline-rush thrill that temporarily soothes the pain. But of course it doesn't last, and it actually makes everything worse. Sexual promiscuity involves self-degradation and guilt, and the pit of depression grows even deeper. This particular behavioral pattern is nearly always the result of depression or low self-esteem, and we have the best results in helping a young lady if we treat the depression rather than the behavior it causes.

> **Boys and girls are both attracted to drug abuse in times of depression.**

Recently, we've also observed an upsurge in female violence.

According to the FBI's Uniform Crime Report, the number of girls ages ten to seventeen arrested for aggravated assault has doubled over the last two decades. One in three juveniles arrested for violent crimes today is female.[3]

Boys and girls are both attracted to drug abuse in times of depression. The reasons are the same ones that cause depressed adults to abuse alcohol. The reason marijuana makes a dangerous combination with depression is that it actually blocks the pain for a brief period. It is not an antidepressant, however—just a temporary balm that makes depression feel worse afterward. Then the teenager must find a greater high, which could mean larger doses or more dangerous drugs. If you were to find your teenager involved in drugs, you might get drug treatment for her. It would seem the natural thing to do. But the root cause might well be depression, and this behavior, or some other that is equally destructive, will always be present until the true disease is confronted.

## Mild, Moderate, and Severe Depression

Your teenager's depression may be mild and manageable. The crucial thing is that you identify it and address it. Could there be a specific event or situation that has touched off these troubled emotions? Such is often the case with mild depression. Your family's move to a new neighborhood or town could lurk behind it. Problems in the family, particularly between Mom and Dad, can bring about mild depression in a teenager.

We often fail to realize how painful some changes can be for our children. When Pat and I visited our daughter, Carey, during her first year away at college, we went out for ice cream with a big group of her friends. Many of the students mentioned how much they missed their homes, their siblings, and their parents. They couldn't understand why they received so few letters or phone calls. I'm certain the folks they missed had no idea of the severity of the homesickness in these young people.

Yet some parents pick that precise time to separate or divorce, naively believing it's the most sensible time. The teenager has built his foundation of security in their parents and his home, and both of these are suddenly lost to him.

In moderate and severe depression, a teenager begins to lose his ability to think clearly, logically, and rationally. He begins to filter all that he sees and experiences through the prism of his hurt, disappointment, and distress. Therefore the world becomes completely bleak to him, and there is no telling him otherwise. Counseling becomes extremely difficult, because reasoning is ineffective. There is a danger that the teenager will act out his depression unless professional caregivers are consulted. Depression does not run its course. It does not fade away. It must be confronted and cured by those who love the sufferer.

## Eating Disorders

Mary Pipher's book *Reviving Ophelia* deals with the pain of today's adolescent girls. She writes that the narrow definition of a female in our culture is a "poisoning" factor for our young women. Girls continue to be victims of abuse, self-mutilation, consumerism, and media pressure to conform to others' ideals.[4] Pipher writes:

> With early adolescence, girls surrender their relaxed attitudes
> about their bodies and take up the burden of self-criticism. Just
> at the point their hips are becoming rounder and they are gain-
> ing fat cells, they see magazines and movies or hear remarks by

peers that suggest to them that their bodies are all wrong. Many girls scorn their true body and work for a false body. They allow the culture to define who they should be.[5]

In our culture women between the ages of twelve and twenty-five are victims of eating disorders. These disorders are characterized by a preoccupation with weight that results in severe disturbances in eating and other behaviors. These disorders include:

## Anorexia Nervosa

Essentially self-starvation, this disorder involves a refusal to maintain a minimally normal body weight. In severe cases anorexia can be life-threatening. Complications from anorexia nervosa tragically brought about the death of singer Karen Carpenter.

## Bulimia Nervosa

Bulimia is the most common eating disorder among young women. It involves repeated episodes of binge eating followed by various episodes of purging the body of food and any possible weight gain. It's possible to have a normal weight and still suffer from bulimia, so we can't draw conclusions simply from someone's physical appearance.

## Binge Eating

This is characterized by frequent episodes of overeating without purging. In this case, perhaps 40 percent of the sufferers are male, while it has been reported that as many as one in five young women report having had a binge relationship with food.[6]

Eating disorders are serious business. While professional help is warranted, the real solution begins in the mind and heart. Parents can help prevent their teenage child from falling victim to an eating disorder by giving her plenty of love and building her self-concept. Help your teenager—particularly your girl—understand that she is not her appearance.

> **Parents can help prevent their teenage children from falling victim to eating disorders by giving them plenty of love and building their self-concept.**

Good health does call for an appropriate body weight, of course, but we need to help our teenagers see through the lies and deceit that Hollywood and Madison Avenue foist upon us concerning who is or is not a "beautiful person."

"We are God's workmanship" (Ephesians 2:10). That means he loves us perfectly even if we come into this world with minds susceptible to ADHD, bodies genetically predisposed to being too thin or too plump, or spirits given to anxiety. We can do all things through him because he strengthens us (see Philippians 4:13). We are not special because of our appearances but because of our spiritual birthright. We are children of God, he loves us, and he intends to do great and wonderful things through each of us.

A wise parent today will take careful note of a child's relationship to food. Food is a good thing, given for our nutrition and enjoyment. But it can be abused as surely as any narcotic. Some teenagers put too much emphasis on food because they have learned to do so from their parents. You may have to begin by examining your own dietary habits.

Families have great success in working together toward a healthy diet. I recommend that every parent reflect on dietary approaches in his or her home, and make a goal toward a healthier and more wholesome lifestyle. Be certain your teenager continues to get an annual medical examination, and if weight fluctuates too much above or below the normal range for that age, ask your doctor for help.

## ADD and ADHD

There has been an explosion of awareness about attention deficit disorder (ADD) and attention-deficit hyperactivity disorder (ADHD) in recent times. While these terms and their implications are very complex, they are widely known in our world today. We can be grateful that there is more understanding and more help for teenagers who suffer from these disorders. Another positive consideration is that there is an extremely high correlation between ADHD and creativity. Therefore, the "curse" nearly always comes packaged with a blessing—in the ability to achieve great things artistically, musically, and in many other fields. As a matter of fact, I'm hesitant to call these behaviors "disorders." It just happens that certain bright, perceptive people fit less comfortably into the way classrooms and the world tend to be structured.

Since there are so many similarities between ADD and ADHD, I consider them together here. They seem to be caused by an imbalance or deficiency in certain chemicals that regulate the efficiency with which the brain controls behavior. And they both involve two neurological problems: perceptual difficulties and short attention span. ADHD adds another wrinkle: hyperactivity. However, hyperactivity and short attention span are very close in nature, so they can be taken together for our discussion.

In children, ADHD is characterized by impulsive behavior, rest-lessness, and inattentiveness to external direction. The behavior isn't always "hyper," however—it can be quite the opposite. During the adolescent period we see a transition in how ADD/ADHD affects the person. The problem becomes more of an inability to structure life and plan simple daily tasks. Inattentiveness and restlessness are no longer the main problems—only secondary ones.

Your teenager will have struggled for many years just to focus on classroom activities or on any one area of importance else-where. She will have trouble organizing her homework regimen or the contents of her bedroom. Distraction is her ever-present enemy. She may have come to mistakenly perceive that she is rest-less, careless, lazy, or clumsy. Even with greater public recognition of the symptoms, people usually will not realize the underlying physiological causes.

Two particular problems between a parent and an ADHD child are that the teenager is too restless to receive the love a parent tries to give, and the parent ends up focusing on behavior rather than needs. The parent is drawn into the trap of becoming impatient, weary of the problems, and expressing negative feelings to the teenager. Therefore the teenager, angry at herself and *her* parent, feels unloved. She acts out her anger through even more difficult behavior and receives yet more negative expression from the parent. An ADD/ADHD sufferer may experience terrible feelings of worthless-ness and low self-esteem and a crippling sense of not being accepted by parents, teachers, and others. The cycle can be very difficult to break, but parents must redouble their determination that their love be *unconditional*, based on who the child is rather than how she behaves. Some of our children simply have minds that work in a different way and, therefore, behavior that is different. They're trying their best, and they deserve all our love and encouragement.

Otherwise, the cycle can spread to other problems. We see an example here of how disorders may overlap, because the teenager will surely suffer from intense anxiety and possibly slide into depression. Assuming a clear diagnosis, a medication such as methylphenidate (known as Ritalin, Metadate, or Methylin) can make a difference. Adderall, a mixture of dextroamphetamine and laevoamphetamine salts, is also becoming prevalent among prescriptions. There is an array of new medications either emerging or under development as well. The right one will normalize the attention span, help your teenager feel better about his capabilities and himself, and improve the relationship between parent and child.

There are also coping skills and adaptive behavior that may be helpful, often involving careful arrangement of life to help the ADD/ADHD teenager make the most of things. Above all, keep everything positive as you help your ADD/ADHD teen. Emphasize that special gifts and talents come with this special designation (not disorder). Through the ages, a tremendous proportion of our artists and achievers had the kind of mind we now recognize and label as an ADD/ADHD mind. The challenges and problems can be met with adaptive and medical remedies; the advantages can be enjoyed for many years to come.

## Bullying

Perhaps this is a good place to deal with another phenomenon that has unfortunately gotten out of control in our angry culture: bullying. This behavior is as old as the aggression in the human spirit, of course, but it stands to reason that when a culture of children is angry, it manifests more abusive behavior.

Bullying can be harmful whether it comes in psychological or physical forms. Teenagers are naturally very sensitive about various issues: appearance, clothing, athletic ability, even the car in which their parents bring them to school. Bullies look for some edge, some angle to assert their dominance over their target. Boys gravitate toward physical bullying while girls tend to use verbal abuse. Did you know that the ancient sport of bullying has now moved into Internet chat rooms and instant-messaging? If a child can be stalked on a cell phone or a computer, it's even harder to find a place of refuge.

> **Bullying can be harmful whether it comes in psychological or physical forms.**

Bullies come most often from homes that have punishment-based discipline. As we know, heavily authoritarian parenting creates anger and the need to establish power in some way, usually through stealth anger. One way to express the anger from home is to bully someone from school or the neighborhood. We also need to consider the aggressor's supporting cast who make the experience more painful: bystanders who don't want to get involved; the bully's accomplices; others who encourage the transgressor. I mention these because it's important to teach your teenager to do all he can to work against the bullying he sees around him. He wouldn't want to realize that he is adding to the pain of an oppressed child even by standing back and watching.

If your child is shy, anxious, insecure, or lacking in social skills, she may make a good target for bullying. If she doesn't have the "perfect" body shape or clothing, these factors could be added. A child who is being bullied will grow far more negative in her attitude toward school. She'll tend to feign illness frequently as a way of staying home. Please be aware that being the object of bullying is terribly painful, even when it isn't physical. It's humiliating and degrading to a teenager at a particularly vulnerable time. Also realize that much of the time our teenagers won't make us aware of what is going on, even when the pain becomes intense. They feel there's not much that can be done about it, or that adult intervention will make things worse, or that their parents will tell them just to ignore it because it's a normal part of life.

Let your child know that it's always right to come to you and tell you about his concerns. Emphasize to her that the bullying is not her fault, but someone else's emotional problem. Since your teenager will feel dehumanized and rather helpless, do all that you can to bolster her self-esteem. That means avoiding a "Don't worry, I'll handle everything" approach. Instead, involve your teenager in any solution. Ask her what she thinks should and should not be done. Be very sensitive to her feelings toward any remedies you take.

This is one more reason to have windows of communication wide open between you and your teen. Look and listen closely to the signals, which aren't always verbal or direct. Ask vague but leading questions ("Any problems today?") that will give your teenager an opportunity to tell you what you need to know. Talk to other parents and see what additional information sifts through concerning your teenager's social world.

To make the external situation better, check into your school's policies against bullying; many schools are now working in that direction. You may need to apply a little pressure to principals and teachers, holding them accountable to be more aware of what goes on in the gym, the locker room, the hallway, or the cafeteria. If a physical attack occurs, notify the police.

## Words of Hope

The problems of this chapter must be taken seriously but calmly. You can be certain that you are surrounded by many other people in your church and your community who face the same challenges. You also have a tremendous advantage if you can simply recognize the symptoms and identify the true enemy. Most of the real damage is done because people fail to realize a problem or a disorder is present—whether it is depression, bulimia, or bullying—and then attack the symptoms. This is a self-defeating cycle.

In the case of your teenager, remember that if love casts out all fear, as the Bible tells us, it is also the one great medicine for every problem we can ever experience—which is not to say we won't use the other remedies we have discussed here. The point is that in the absence of a loving home, every problem can only grow worse and more powerful; with a foundation of unconditional support, there is no problem you cannot overcome. Fill your teenager's emotional tank, be closely involved in her personal world, and make unconditional love the foundation of your relationship. *Keep very close emotional communication at all times.* These actions alone will make your home tremendously healthy and positive. If there are chemical

> **Keep very close emotional communication at all times.**

causes involved, medicine and professional counseling can make a wonderful difference.

Finally, consider these words from the New Testament, written by James:

> Consider it pure joy, my brothers, whenever you face trials of many kinds, because you know that the testing of your faith develops perseverance. Perseverance must finish its work so that you may be mature and complete, not lacking anything. If any of you lacks wisdom, he should ask God, who gives generously to all without finding fault, and it will be given to him. (James 1:2–5)

Dear parent, there are treasures within those brief sentences. There is treasure in the knowledge that your family's struggles are not without meaning. God does not cause them, but he takes hold of them and uses them to make each member of your family stronger and wiser. We grow the most through our problems and our suffering, and we become closer to the mature, complete creations he wants us to be. Two things are required of us to gain this treasure: perseverance and faith.

There is treasure also in the promise that God will generously give you wisdom. He may give it through your reading and study about these challenges. He may give it through the intervention of a skilled physician or counselor. He may give it through your own growth and prayer as you grow closer in dependence on him. One thing is required of you to gain this treasure: ask. I've never known God to turn away when I've asked for his help, and I know you'll find the same wonderful resource in his love.

## 12

# gifts to the future

MY WIFE, PAT, AND I SAW THREE AMAZING CHILDREN COME through our home—two sons and a daughter. We watched their determined journeys toward knowledge, capability, and independence, from their first tentative steps to those bittersweet moments when they left home to begin their own families. Parents, having done the greatest part of their work, find themselves left with wonderful memories and, hopefully, a few terrific grandchildren.

We think back about the trials and the triumphs of parenting. So much learning occurred the hard way, but we did some things right too. Pat and I glow with pride as we show others our snapshots of three successful young adults—our children—and the promising families they are building on their own. It's delightful to see ways my children have learned so well to manage anger; I could now learn a lesson or two from them.

And we realize more than ever what it meant when we planted the seeds for the harvest we're now enjoying. As parents, most of the time we have no idea we're planting anything at all. But it goes on every day of a family's life: a stray comment here, a word of instruction there, a key example lived out somewhere else. You'll be startled by the lessons your children will recall for you one day as you share memories. The way you respected your own parents, for example, will have made a great impression; the regard you had for the members of your adult Sunday school class; your feelings about patriotism of civic duties. In tiny details and deeply significant subjects alike, your children will have absorbed a lifetime of wisdom, and in turn they will transmit those legacies to your grandchildren.

> You'll be startled by the lessons your children will recall for you one day as you share memories.

We ponder a great deal the passing on of heirlooms of jewelry, real estate, or family china. Shouldn't we spend that much more time thinking about these far more precious legacies: those involving how we live our lives? In this final chapter I wish to leave you with a list of "seedlings of grace" that I hope you are even now planting in the living garden of your family life.

## Are You Leaving a Legacy of Good Thinking?

It's so important that our young people learn to think rationally, logically, and sequentially. We send them out into the world just as Jesus sent the disciples: as sheep among wolves, hopefully as wise as serpents yet as harmless as doves (see Matthew 10:16). They must think clearly to understand how the world works. They must think clearly to perceive the difference between right and wrong in every decision. They must think clearly to develop socially and function among others with integrity and character. And finally, they must think clearly to be able to apply our ancient spiritual faith to a modern and ever-changing world.

So many adults today lack the ability to think clearly. We see this wherever we go. Teenagers begin—only *begin*—to think rationally at age fifteen. At this point he begins to use his own mind and reasoning processes. That ability will grow and become more accurate as you gently, positively provide the guidance. Many parents only dispute or correct their teenager, and he doesn't feel he has received respect. When put on the defensive, anyone is more likely to irrationally hang on to faulty reasoning.

Demonstrate to your teenager how to think through an issue. Here's an example from my own experience. Our son David wanted to watch a television show of which Pat and I didn't approve. His reasoning, typical for a teen, was that there was no violence on the show. "Maybe not," I said, "but the show is hedonistic and narcissistic." David was immediately curious about those terms, so I asked him to bring the dictionary (always a great tool for intellectually training your teenagers). He soon understood my point—that the show glorified personal pleasure and self-centeredness. Since he helped work all this out

> **Demonstrate to your teenager how to think through an issue.**

with a dictionary, he learned something about reasoning and discernment.

Leave your teenager a legacy of sharp, clear-minded thinking, and he will be so much better equipped to deal with the decisions he must face. But as you do so, make sure your teaching is gentle, loving, and respectful. Use humor and the teenager's curiosity, and someday you'll see him applying the same kind of reasoning to adult decisions.

## Are You Leaving a Legacy of an Open Home?

We still know and talk to a considerable number of our children's friends. As young adults, they've come to us for advice just as our children have. Why? Because we got to know them, and they have happy memories of our home. We worked carefully and intentionally to build a home environment in which our children would enjoy spending time, and where their friends would want to come as well.

> When teenagers have an unpleasant home situation, they spend every possible moment somewhere else—and therefore are more likely to end up with bad influences and in bad places.

I can't emphasize enough the importance of taking this step, because it causes several good things to happen. For one, there is more opportunity for you to supervise your teenager and observe the friends he has selected. When teenagers have an unpleasant home situation, they spend every possible moment somewhere else—and therefore are more likely to end up with bad influences and in bad places.

There are a number of steps you can take to "build a better mousetrap" for teenagers. You can keep a nice family room and perhaps an outdoor area that teens will enjoy. Let them know they're always welcome to bring their friends home. Make it a habit to have cookouts and the kind of simple dinners where a friend or two can stay for the meal. Keep appropriate videos and DVDs around, along with board games or any kind of wholesome entertainment your teenager's friends would enjoy. Above all else, be the kind of parent to whom your child will want to introduce his friends. That means being friendly and open, engaged and interested, affirming and generous. You will be more than amazed at how positively your teenager's friends will respond, because so many of them crave a stable, happy, and loving home environment. Too few of them have approachable, affirming parents who make eye contact and give focused attention. And if you have a good listening ear, they will bring their problems and questions to you. Your own teenager is bound to be delighted by the respect his friends will have for you.

Jesus called us the "light of the world" and "a city on a hill" (Matthew 5:14). That's a good metaphor for a loving Christian home during times of turmoil in our world and its families. A city on a hill cannot be hidden, and young people will flock to your home. God will work through you to bless their lives. As our Father does with all good things, he will multiply the impact of your parenting to those within the reach of your home. What greater legacy could you leave your teenager than a sanctuary of wisdom and guidance for his friends?

## Are You Leaving a Legacy of Ministry and Compassion?

Young people today know all about the importance of career and success. They are saturated with that ethic. Many of them have two working parents who have made great sacrifices toward the goal of salary and career advancement, usually in the name of providing for their family.

But do we want our children to be budding workaholics? Do we want their lives to be out of balance, tilted toward accomplishment and lacking in relationships? Furthermore, what are they learning about our responsibility to a needy world? In the passage above, in which Jesus told us we are a city set on a hill, he also said we are the salt of the earth. That means we are here to make others thirsty for the living water that only Jesus can provide. There is so much wrong with our world, but God still loves every inhabitant on this planet. There is so much sin and corruption around us, but God wants us to do more about it than simply build walls of protection. He wants us to venture outside those walls and be part of the solution.

When was the last time your family engaged in some kind of community service project together? What would it do for your family to go on a mission trip together this summer? Imagine the blessing of building closer family bonds even as you have the satisfaction of serving needy people. Many people are reporting today that nothing has been better for their family's closeness than taking the family overseas to help build a medical facility, or simply to work in a soup kitchen downtown. Teenagers have a sense of adventure, and their souls can be touched forever when you take them outside the confines of the high school hallway or the Scout hut and show them true human need.

Does your family support a missionary? A needy child? These simple expressions of God's love and encouragement will make a powerful impact on the young minds and hearts in your family. Again, you will leave a legacy of lighting a candle in a dark world, rather than simply huddling together to shut out the darkness. Your gift to the present is an even better gift to the future.

## A Brief, Shining Moment

Stop and think about how fast the time has gone. Doesn't it seem like yesterday that your teen entered the world? It goes far too fast, and that includes the time between now and the day your teenager leaves the nest.

There's no way to accurately describe the little feeling in the pit of a parent's stomach when a teenager packs his belongings and takes off to seek his fortune. We find ourselves pausing by his old bedroom, which now seems a little empty and sad. We find ourselves valuing snapshots and phone calls and e-mail more than we ever expected. Once we pleaded for our children to give us a moment's peace; now we pray they'll give us a few more moments of their time.

> The day your teenager leaves your care may be a little bittersweet, but it's also a day of victory.

The day your teenager leaves your care may be a little bittersweet, but it's also a day of victory. You've made it through the minefield of adolescence, and—if you've been an attentive parent, offering plenty of unconditional love—I predict you'll be quite happy with the fruit of your labor. That fruit will be a teenager who is balanced, energetic, gifted, filled with integrity and spiritual values, and ready to make an impact on the world. Then we realize that we only clutched our children to us for one brief, shining moment in the great span of time. But how important was that moment? How many lessons were taught and absorbed? How many potential problems were headed off and healed? How many obstacles were overcome? No wonder you're a little tired! Good parenting is hard work, but in the end, the reward is worth the labor and the weariness.

Again, on that day I hope you won't feel empty or alone when your precious child leaves home. I hope you'll realize that you have a Father and a Friend who has been there all along, who counseled you in every crisis, who provided every resource you needed, and who is just as pleased as you with how it all turned out.

My friends, parenting carries a holy blessing because our Lord describes himself, before any other designation, as a Parent. He characterizes us, before any other classification, as his children. And no matter how we grow and change, he never stops being our Father, and we never stop being his children. Nothing can separate us from his love. This is why I believe parenting provides the deepest joy we can experience. We were made in his image, we replenish the earth in imitation of his creation of us, and we train our children in the same way he has trained us. While we carry out many tasks that reflect our creation in his image, what task could draw us closer to his very nature than loving and raising our children?

Therefore, when your son or daughter pulls away in that car and you think, *Please don't go far; please keep in close touch—daily, if possible,* you can know that your heavenly Father has the very same thoughts about you. *Don't go far. Keep in close touch—daily, if possible.* Now that you've raised a child, you understand the deep feelings of love and contentment God has for you. And that means though your home may be quiet, the rest of your life will be anything but dull and empty.

I pray you're ready to embrace your task with new excitement, eagerness, and dependence on God. May your adventure in parenting be filled with many delightful surprises.

# five ways to get the most from this book

1. **Down the Block.** Invite neighborhood parents for a weekly discussion over coffee, chapter by chapter. You'll enjoy building relationships on your street—and when the study is complete, your friends will find they've become a parental support group for advice and encouragement.

2. **Over the Weekend.** Have a "Parent Getaway" as a weekend retreat. Hit the book's key points for group sessions, small group interaction, and a closing time of prayer and commitment. A concentrated weekend focus on the material will give it extra impact, and you'll come home refreshed and rejuvenated, ready to apply your new understandings.

3. **In the Classroom.** Study a chapter per week with your adult Sunday school class. *How to Really Parent Your Teenager* can become a practical and rewarding class curriculum. Class members will enjoy comparing notes from their parenting experiences during the week—and reporting the week's progress in applying what they learn.

4. **With Your Spouse.** For a very personal one-on-one study experience, study each chapter with your spouse. Plan and protect an uninterrupted hour once or twice per week for reviewing the chapters and applying them to the special challenges of parenting your teenager. You'll grow together as a couple even as you grow into wiser parenthood.

5. **Over the Internet.** Start a "Really Parenting Teens" bulletin board (such as a Google group or Yahoo group), and invite your friends to log on and share insights as they work through the book. Long after your study is finished, parents will want to continue sharing their experiences and assistance in your Web group.

# study guide

Use this special chapter-by-chapter guide to enhance your growth as a parent. The questions are designed in such a way that you can use them in your personal study, in discussion with your spouse, or in a more formal group-learning experience.

Note the three kinds of questions provided:

1. **Start.** The first question for each chapter is a general (and gentle) way to begin thinking about the chapter's topic. It will help you or your group recall personal experiences that relate to what we'll be discussing. In a group session, this question is a good "icebreaker"—that is, it encourages participants to jump right into the discussion.

2. **Study.** These questions—five or six, usually—move you through the main points of each chapter. Their goal is to help you not only clarify the key ideas, but to begin thinking about how they will help you as a parent.

3. **Strengthen.** Each chapter's final question will motivate you to consider how to put these truths to work in the life of your teenager during the next few days. These may be the most important questions of all. So if you study this book in a group setting, be certain you leave enough time to discuss the *strengthen* question.

# 1 | a stranger in the house

## start

1. As you look over the "road map" at the end of this chapter, which issue of parenting a teen are you most excited about studying? Which are you least excited about? Why?

## study

1. Does your teenager seem like a "stranger" in any of the ways described in this chapter? Why or why not?
2. Which forms of mass media (television, music, movies, computer, etc.) are most powerful in your home for your teenager? For you?
3. Evaluate your teenager's relationship to possessions and materialism on a scale of 1 to 10, with 10 being the most materialistic. Has age made this more or less pervasive?
4. How are honesty and integrity issues in your teenager's world? When was the last time the subject was raised?
5. What aspects of your teenager and his/her friends give you the most optimism? Explain.

## strengthen

1. As you begin this study of parenting teenagers, what areas do you feel you should focus on first? About which three items do you wish to ask God's particular help? Spend a few minutes in prayer and reflection, asking for his guidance during this growth experience.

## 2 | anger: the essential problem

### start

1. What kinds of things made you angry when you were a teenager? How has your relationship to anger changed with maturity?

### study

1. How does Dr. Campbell define *anger*? In what ways can it be a positive thing? Negative?
2. What specific factors make this a particularly angry world? How do those factors enter your own family's life?
3. In what situations should a parent tolerate unpleasant expressions of anger in a younger teen? Why?
4. Why isn't venting a good thing?
5. What is stealth anger? Why is it the most dangerous form of anger?
6. What are some illustrations of "normal" passive-aggressive behavior?

### strengthen

1. Of the practical tips for reacting to your teenager's anger, which one is most helpful? How can you make certain to use one or several of these during the next "crisis"?

## 3 | keys to self-control

### start

1. Most of us have "hot buttons" that make us lose our tempers more rapidly. What are yours?

### study

1. Why is your own self-control so crucial in teaching anger management to your teenager?
2. What can we learn about self-control through the Scripture passages detailed in this chapter?
3. What are the specific issues of body, mind, and spirit that enable us to have mature self-control?
4. In your view, which is the most important or helpful of the "coping" methods mentioned? Why?
5. What is the place of forgiveness in helping our teenagers learn about anger?

### strengthen

1. Spend some time reflecting on your current state of physical, mental, and spiritual health. What can you do to improve each? On a sheet of paper, make three columns (one each for body, mind, and spirit), and list several steps you can take to care for yourself more lovingly.

# 4 | love: the essential solution

## start

1. Why, in your opinion, is love "the essential solution" in parenting and practically every other human problem? What is special about love?

## study

1. Dr. Campbell writes that nearly all parents love their children, but the children too often fail to perceive it. Do you think this is more the fault of parent or child? Explain.
2. In John 13:1, Jesus showed "the full extent of his love." What does that mean? How can a parent do the same?
3. How does typical adult learning differ from that of a teenager?
4. Has anyone ever loved you unconditionally? Discuss how you knew, how it felt, and how it has affected your life.
5. What does "filling the tank" mean? In what ways does your teenager enjoy having his/her tank filled?

## strengthen

1. Review your interactions with your teenager over the last three days. What actions effectively communicated your love to your teenager? Where did you miss an opportunity? Focus on "tank-filling" over the next three days.

## 5 | three ways to show love

### start

1. What was the most emotionally powerful demonstration of love you have ever received? What was the most emotionally powerful demonstration of love you have ever given?

### study

1. Which of the three ways to love do you find most difficult? Which of the three is the most important? Why?
2. Why does a teenager need focused attention?
3. Dr. Campbell used a date with his daughter to illustrate how to best make use of focused time. Which ideas did you find most helpful? How can you apply these ideas to your own situation?
4. In what ways are the eyes "windows to the soul"? How do various members of your family use "eye language"?
5. Why is it so difficult to use physical touch with teenagers? How well do you accomplish it with your teen?

### strengthen

1. Monitor your use of focused attention, eye contact, and physical touch over the next three days. Carefully use an appropriate amount of each. Report on how it affected your interactions with your teenager.

# 6 | discipline with love

## start

1. How was discipline approached when your parents were raising you? How much has this influenced your own approaches to discipline?

## study

1. How would you characterize the current attitudes toward discipline in our society?
2. What are the two dangerous trends in discipline? What is the effect of each?
3. Dr. Campbell says that teenagers appreciate boundaries. Since the reverse often seems true, how would you explain this concept?
4. Why do you think the family dinner table serves as a good indicator of effective families? What would it say about your family?
5. What is the "faithfulness principle," and how does it work?
6. What are some specific ways parents can effectively work together to share information and support?

## strengthen

1. What goals and limits are you setting with your teenager? How are you allowing him/her to earn privileges by demonstrating maturity? Think of some new ways to put this idea into action.

# 7 | protecting your teenager

## start

1. When it comes to protecting your teenager, what possibilities give you the most fear? Why?

## study

1. What are some of the most uncomfortable aspects of teenagers moving into the social realm?

2. Where are some good places to find like-minded parents? What success have you already had in doing so?

3. Why shouldn't parents simply trust their teenagers to handle a demanding or tempting social situation? Explain.

4. In what situations can delay be a helpful strategy?

5. What is your long-range goal in protecting your teenager from harmful influences?

## strengthen

1. What current social situations make you the most uneasy about your teenager? What are some steps you can take to more effectively supervise the influences to which your teenager is exposed?

# 8 | mind vs. media

## start

1. How do you handle entertainment issues in your family? How do you decide what is or isn't appropriate for your teenager?

## study

1. Describe the "systematic rebelliousness" that is reflected in much of the media targeted at teenagers today. What are some recent examples you have observed?

2. What steps can a parent take to make the Internet safe within a home? Have you done so?

3. What is the role of television within your home? What are some programs your family avoids?

4. What is the connection between cultural media and teenage fatigue? What kinds of family policies can help this situation?

5. What are some ways to turn movies, TV shows, music, and other media into learning experiences?

## strengthen

1. What cultural media seem most important to your teenager? If you feel there are unhealthy influences coming through, what can you do to better supervise your teenager's activities?

## 9 | beyond the birds and the bees

### start

1. Discuss some ways the dynamics of sex education have changed from the time of your adolescence until now.

### study

1. What helpful messages are teenagers giving us about the place of parents in the issue of sexual involvement?
2. How would you summarize the Bible's approach to sexuality? In what ways can this most effectively be presented to a teenager?
3. What aspects of our culture are dehumanizing to teenagers in their presentation of sexuality?
4. How can a parent help a teenager prepare for dating?
5. Do you think "gender training" is important? In what ways? How are you taking care of this need?

### strengthen

1. When was your last open discussion of sexuality with your teenager? What future moment might offer a good opportunity?

# 10 | teaching values

## start

1. When you were a teenager, what was your spiritual perception? How did you view God? How did you view church?

## study

1. How is cheating in school a spiritual issue? How can we teach integrity?
2. Why do you think the 20/80 percentages on cheating/not cheating have reversed during the last few decades?
3. What kinds of attitudes are the best for our teenagers to absorb around the house? How can this be better accomplished in your home?
4. What insights did you gather from the Deuteronomy 11:18–21 passage about teaching?
5. In what physiological ways is early adolescence so important for the formation of values?
6. What are the most important guidelines for training our teenagers in the matter of churchmanship?

## strengthen

1. List the various ways spiritual training is occurring in your home. In what ways can you make it more intentional?

# 11 | anxiety, depression, and other challenges

## start

1. What were your greatest fears as a teenager? What do you expect might be your teenager's greatest fears?

## study

1. Do you believe there are more behavioral disorders today, or are we simply more aware of them through science? Explain your answer.

2. What is the most important thing you can do to help your teenager keep fear at bay?

3. How can a parent help a teenager deal with anxiety?

4. What are the different ways boys and girls act out depression? Why?

5. Why is it so dangerous when depression goes undetected? What are some possible consequences?

## strengthen

1. Does your teenager face any of the challenges enumerated in this chapter? If not, which would be most likely? How can you build a better awareness of your teenager's basic mental, physical, and spiritual health?

# 12 | gifts to the future

## start

1. If you could have one wish granted for your teenager's future, what would it be?

## study

1. Several legacies for the future are described in this chapter. Which one do you find most striking or compelling? Why?
2. Good, clear thinking should be a given. How can we train our teenagers to be more rational and objective?
3. How can your home be perceived as a safe and fun place for your teenager to bring his/her friends?
4. When has your family served your community or gone on a mission trip together? How might this be a powerful experience to plan?

## strengthen

1. Spend some time reviewing the chapters of this book. List five concepts that you found most powerful and essential. How will you work them into your parenting? Have a private time of recommitment as a parent, asking God to make each new day a victory in helping you guide your teenager to a successful, mature, and loving life.

# notes

## chapter 1: a stranger in the house

1. George Barna, *Real Teens: A Contemporary Snapshot of Youth Culture* (Ventura, CA: Regal, 2001).

2. "Christmas: The Growing Backlash Against Greed," *The Week*, December 10, 2004, cited at www.preachingtoday.com.

3. American College of Emergency Physicians, June 2003, http://www.acep.org.

4. James Patterson and Peter Kim, *The Day America Told the Truth* (New York: Prentice Hall, 1991), 6.

5. Ibid., 45.

6. Associated Press survey, cited at http://www.nysscpa.org/home/2002/102/3week/article6.htm.

## chapter 2: anger: the essential problem

1. "Controlling Anger—Before It Controls You," c. 2005, American Psychological Association, Office of Public Affairs.

2. "Inside the Teenage Brain," written, produced, and directed by Sarah Spinks (PBS Frontline television program), aired January 31, 2002.

3. R. H. Hornberger, "The differential reduction of aggressive responses as a function of interpolated activities." *American Psychologist,* 1959, 14, 354.

## chapter 3: keys to self-control

1. August 26, 2004, news conference with Louis Kincannon, director, U.S. Census Bureau; and Daniel H. Weinberg, Ph.D., chief, Housing and Household Economic Statistics, U.S. Census Bureau; Commonwealth Fund statement.

2. Harriet B. Braiker, "The Power of Self-Talk," *Psychology Today,* December 1989.

## chapter 5: three ways to show love

1. Proceedings of the National Academy of Sciences 2002, cited at http://www.ananova.com.

2. "Child's Play," MacNeil/Lehrer Productions, televised May 29, 1997.

3. Daniel Goleman, "The Experience of Touch: Research Points to a Critical Role," *New York Times,* February 2, 1988.

## chapter 6: discipline with love

1. Shari Roan, "Author blames obesity rates on food habits," *Los Angeles Times*, October 1, 1997, cited at http://www.chron.com/content/chronicle/features/97/10/02/obesity-rate.0-0.html.

2. "The Unofficial Official Rules of Calvinball," from Bill Watterson's comic strip *Calvin and Hobbes* and cites at http://bartel.org/calvinball.

3. Patricia Hersch, *A Tribe Apart: A Journey into the Heart of American Adolescence* (New York: Fawcett Columbine, 1998).

4. Ibid., 19.

5. *Teens and Their Parents in the 21st Century: An Examination of Trends in Teen Behavior and the Role of Parental Involvement*, a report by the President's Council of Economic Advisers, May 2, 2000, 2.

6. Ibid., 3.

7. "An Interview with Larry Crabb," *Discipleship Journal* 44 (Colorado Springs: NavPress, c. 1999).

## chapter 7: protecting your teenager

1. Chap Clark, *Hurt: Inside the World of Today's Teenagers* (Grand Rapids: Baker Academic, 2004).

2. Ibid., 21.

3. Ibid., 171.

4. "Coed Sleepovers Increasingly Common," *Milwaukee Sentinel-Journal*, September 4, 2002. Also cited at http://www.jsonline.com/news/nat/ap/sep02/ap-coed-sleepovers090402.asp.

## chapter 8: mind vs. media

1. "Tell the FCC to Stop Cutting Deals with CBS," http://www.afa.net/videos/withoutatrace.asp.

2. Ibid.

3. "Students Selling Drugs: Who's at Risk?" http://www.kidshealth.org/research/students_selling_drugs.html.

4. Study by Stanford and Duquesne Universities, cited in *U.S. News and World Report*, March 27, 2000.

5. London School of Economics, January 2002.

6. Steve Rabey, "Hunks and Hotties Hooking Up," *Youthworker Journal*, September/October 2004, also cited at http://www.youthspecialties.com/articles/topics/culture/hunks.php.

7. New York University Communications Professor Mark Crispin-Miller, quoted on PBS Frontline documentary, "Merchants of Cool, " first broadcast February 27, 2001.

8. Study published by *Sexual Addiction & Compulsivity: The Journal of Treatment & Prevention*, cited at http://www.thencsp.com/pornfacts.htm.

9. For much of the information in this section, the author is indebted to the excellent summary by Marilyn Miller, "Teenagers and Internet Safety," found at http://www.methuen.k12.ma.us/cgs/teenagers_and_internet_safety.htm.

10. For an additional helpful list of things parents can do to protect their children on the Internet, see http://www.icra.org/parents/parentsguide.

11. B. J. Wilson, D. Kunkel, D. Linz, J. Potter, E. Donnerstein, S. L. Smith, E. Blumenthal, and M. Berry, "Violence in Television Programming Overall," in Center for Communication and Social Policy, *National Television Violence Study*, vol. 2 (Thousand Oaks, CA: Sage, 1997), 3–204.

12. You'll find more information on RIAA ratings at http://www.riaa.com/issues/parents/advisory.asp#faq.

13. Dr. Mary Carskadon, quoted in "Inside the Teenage Brain" (PBS).

14. The National Sleep Foundation, quoted at http://www.speakingofhealth.com/features/sleeptipsforteens.html.

## chapter 9: beyond the birds and the bees

1. PBS Frontline special, "The Lost Children of Rockdale County," http://www.worldnetdaily.com/news/article.asp?ARTICLE_ID=36769.

2. Surveys cited by the National Campaign to Prevent Teen Pregnancy.

3. Ibid.

4. Report on NPR *Morning Edition*, May 21, 2003.

5. News release from RAND Corporation, September 7, 2004. Full research results available at ttp://pediatrics.aappublications.org/cgi/content/full/114/3/e280.

6. Quoted at http://www.rand.org/news/press.04/09.07.html.

7. Ibid.

8. Steve Rabey, "Hunks and Hotties Hooking Up," from *Youthworker Journal*, text available at http://www.youthspecialties.com.

9. Julie Scelfo, "Bad Girls Go Wild," *Newsweek*, June 13, 2005, 67.

10. Ibid., 66.

11. Philip Van Munching, *Boys Will Put You on a Pedestal (So They Can Look Up Your Skirt): A Dad's Advice for Daughters* (New York: Simon & Schuster, 2005), 62.

## chapter 10: teaching values

1. Cited by the Heartland Institute at http://www.heartland.org/Article.cfm?artId=14378.

2. Ibid.

3. Ibid.

4. http://www.josephsoninstitute.org/Survey2004/2004reportcard_press release.htm.

5. Rebecca Grace, "Southern Baptists Still Pondering Public School Exodus," *American Family Association Journal*, August 2004, cited at http://www.directory.crosswalk.com/news/1281480.html.
6. Cited at http://www.christianitytoday.com/le/2004/001/13.7.html.
7. Cited at http://www.barna.org/FlexPage.aspx?Page=Topic&TopicID=10.

## chapter 11: anxiety, depression, and other challenges
1. Cited at http://www.about-teen-depression.com/depression-statistics.html.
2. Marilyn Elias, "Childhood Depression," USA Today, August 13, 1998, 2D.
3. Scelfo, "Bad Girls Go Wild," 66.
4. Mary Pipher, *Reviving Ophelia* (New York: Ballantine), 1994.
5. Ibid., 57.
6. Carolyn Costin, *The Eating Disorder Sourcebook : A Comprehensive Guide to the Causes, Treatments, and Prevention of Eating Disorders* (Los Angeles: Lowell House, 1996), 15.